29 95

60 Q

Building Code
Quick Reference Guide

A Schematic
Building
Design
Timesaver

William J. Brummett
Alec W. Johnson

Professional Publications, Inc.
Belmont, CA

Other Books from Professional Publications, Inc.

Architecture/Interior Design

Architecture Exam Review Volume I: Structural Topics
Architecture Exam Review Volume II: Non-Structural Topics
Architecture Exam Review: Sample Building and Site Design Exam Problems
Interior Design Reference Manual: A Guide to the NCIDQ Exam

Civil/Structural Engineering

Civil Engineering Reference Manual
Civil Engineering Quick Reference Cards
Civil Engineering Sample Examination
Civil Engineering Review Course on Cassettes
Seismic Design of Building Structures
Seismic Design Fast
Timber Design for the Civil P.E. Exam
Fundamentals of Reinforced Masonry Design
246 Solved Structural Engineering Problems

Printed in the United States of America

ISBN: 0-912045-58-2

Library of Congress Catalog Card Number: 92–81992

Professional Publications, Inc.
1250 Fifth Avenue, Belmont, CA 94002
(415) 593-9119

Current printing of this edition (last number): 6 5 4 3 2 1

Contents

Contents

There have been a number of good friends and valued colleagues who have contributed to the effort of creating this book. Their support has helped turn an idea into a reality.

Bob and Billie Benson and Edward Caruana of The Benson Architectural Group offered their support, time, and experience throughout the two-year process of completing this project. Their understanding and unending patience provided the environment that allowed this book to prosper.

Martinez Freeman provided his computer expertise at critical moments in the manuscript's development and production.

A number of editors offered objective reviews and incisive comments which helped strengthen and clarify the manuscript. Among those were David Kent Ballast, AIA, and Larry A. Paul, AIA. Their expert advice was highly valued.

The authors wish to acknowledge the contributions of those above and express our appreciation and gratitude.

Disclaimer

The *Building Code Quick Reference Guide* is intended for preliminary and schematic design, analysis, and programming. It is not intended nor recommended as a replacement for thorough code analysis prior to any phase of documentation beyond preliminary.

Addit.	Additional	**Max.**	Maximum
Adj.	Adjacent	**Min.**	Minimum
Admin.	Administration	**N.A.**	Not allowed
Bldg.	Building	**No.**	Number
Const.	Construction	**Non-combust.**	Non-combustible (construction)
Corr.	Corridor	**Occ.**	Occupant(s)
Cu. ft.	Cubic feet	**Park'g.**	Parking
Dist.	Distance	**P/L**	Property line
Ea.	Each	**Req'd.**	Required
Ext.	Exterior	**Sq. ft.**	Square foot/feet
Exting.	Extinguishing	**Struct.**	Structure/structural
Fire-resist.	Fire-resistive	**Sty.**	Story
F.R.	Fire-resistive (construction)	**UBC**	*Uniform Building Code*
Flr.	Floor	**UPC**	*Uniform Plumbing Code*
Fm.	From	**W/**	With
Gyp. bd.	Gypsum board	**W/in**	Within
Hr.	Hour	<	Less than
Hrs.	Hours	>	Greater than
H.T.	Heavy-timber (construction)	≤	Less than or equal to
Int.	Interior	≥	Greater than or equal to
Lbs.	Pounds	"	Same as above

The practice of architecture and its related professional building trades has become, like most professions, increasingly complex and competitive. To survive in today's business climate, the practitioner must be a competent designer, business person, marketer, contractor, and code expert. Efficiency in these roles is essential to success. This book is designed as a tool, making the necessary task of code research very efficient.

The *Building Code Quick Reference Guide* compiles all the necessary building code information required for schematic and preliminary design, including building square footage and height, fire-resistive requirements, exiting requirements, barrier-free access guidelines, and parking design guidelines, and reorganizes it into a format that is most valuable for architects and building professionals. This expedient format enables a typical two- to four-hour code research for a complex building to be accurately completed in fifteen to twenty minutes. Furthermore, cross-comparison of different construction types can be accomplished easily, yielding clear and evident findings. The decision of which construction type to employ for a given project can thus be made with greater control and understanding.

Although written specifically for preliminary design and analysis, the *Building Code Quick Reference Guide* is also very useful for locating specific regulations within the UBC as questions arise during later phases of design/documentation. Each figure or subject derived from the UBC is accompanied by its UBC section number, for such further investigation.

Those who will find this book valuable are not only architects and designers but engineers, design-build contractors, construction and facility managers, and sophisticated developers and property owners. The *Building Code Quick Reference Guide* allows the legal/codified limits and opportunities of building projects to be ascertained and compared quickly and easily.

Structure of the Guide

The book is divided into three parts and appendices. Part I includes information on occupancy; light, ventilation and sanitation; and building separations. Most of this information is presented in tables or matrices for easiest reference. Part II, "Exiting," combines a concise table with written and graphic information. Both Part I and Part II are derived from the information in the 1991 (latest edition) UBC. Any exceptions or derivations to the information taken from the UBC are noted in this book, either within the tables, in footnotes, or within the text. Information in Part I and Part II is relative for any building project under the jurisdiction of a governing body that has adopted the UBC as its building code (see Figure I.1, page 2).

Part III, "Barrier-free Access," is presented chiefly in graphic form for comprehension. This information is primarily a distillation of the information in the Federal Americans With Disabilities Act (ADA) of 1990.

The brief appendices offer preliminary site design information which most often impacts building design and programming, such as parking and grading requirements.

Effective Use of the Guide

Copy and use the "Code Research Checklist" provided on page 5. It is the most efficient method of using this book and provides a format for a written record of research findings. Using the checklist also allows for effective comparison of construction types for a given project.

The graphic portions of this book are best used either to set programming parameters or alongside the drawing board/computer during design.

Figure I.1

States where the UBC is adopted as the primary building code.
(Consult the local governing agency for any variations or deviations.)

Scope of the Guide

As noted, the *Building Code Quick Reference Guide* is intended for preliminary design and covers all such pertinent material. It is important to note, however, that specific data such as structural, seismic, and construction components/assemblies information is not within the scope of this book and is best derived directly from the regulatory source.

The practical result of using this book is the quick and accurate completion of analysis and preliminary design proposals. Such a savings in time represents opportunity. For those so inclined, the apportionment of less time to pragmatics allows greater effort and energy to be given to more meaningful design considerations.

1. Determine Building Occupancy
(See Table OD.1, page 10.)

2. Determine Building Construction Type
(See Table CT.1, page 11.)

Two approaches to research based on construction type:

a. **The construction type is fixed/given:** Complete the checklist (see step 3) for the selected given occupancy and construction type.

b. **The construction type is not yet determined/ fixed:** Compare types within the occupancy. Completing checklists for a number of construction types will reveal the implications of selecting one construction type over another.

3. Complete the Checklist
(See Code Research Checklist, pages 5–9.)

Photocopy this checklist for use:

    —in comparing results of research

    —in subsequent projects

    —as a concise written record

The checklist works as follows:

a. **Checklist COLUMN headings:**
Information: Record the information found in the guide in this column.

Reference: All information derived from the UBC is accompanied by its UBC section number (i.e., [510]). Record this section number in this column for quick reference if further investigation is desired at a later time.

Notes: Record any footnote information, exceptions, or other pertinent information in this column.

b. **Checklist ROW headings:**
Square footage, building height, and construction: All this information can be found within the occupancy tables found in Chapters 1–6. Each table covers one occupancy.

Light, ventilation, and sanitation: This information is found at the end of each occupancy group. The "Light, Ventilation, and Sanitation" sections include UBC requirements, minimum number of fixtures required to meet barrier-free access requirements, and UPC recommendations for number of fixtures.

Exiting: This information is found in Chapter 8.

Local governing agency requirements: This portion of the checklist is provided for recording any additional regulations set forth by the agency that will be approving/issuing a permit for the project.

4. Consult Barrier-Free Access Guidelines Chapter
Chapter 9 is designed to be used as a graphic reference tool during programming, schematic design, and preliminary design.

5. Consult Appendix
The appendices consolidate the site design requirements that can greatly affect building programming and building design.

Using the Occupancy Tables

(A)

	For 1 Story Buildings[1] [5C]	2 Side Yards >20' Add 1 1/4% Per Foot Over 20'[2] [506a]	3 Side Yards >20' Add 2 1/2% Per Foot Over 20'[2] [506a]	All Side Yards >20' Add 5% Per Foot Over 20'[2] [506a]	Additional Sq. Ft. If Sprinklered[3] [506c]	Maximum Building Height[4] [5D,507]	CONSTRUCTION (FIRE-RESISTIVE REQUIREMENTS IN HOURS)											
							Exterior Bearing Walls [17A]	Interior Bearing Walls [17A]	Exterior Non-bear-ing Walls	Structural Frame [17A]	Permanent Partitions [17A]	Shaft Enclosures [17A]	Floors/ Ceilings [17A]	Roofs/ Ceilings [17A]	Exterior Doors & Windows	Area Separation Walls[10] [505f]	Exit Corridors [3305g]	Exit Stairways [3306l]
Type I	Unlimited	Unlimited	Unlimited	Unlimited	Unlimited	Unlimited	4 hr.	3 hr.	1 hr., <20' fm. p/l 2 hr., <5' fm. p/l 4 hr.[6]	3 hr.	1 hr.	2 hr.	2 hr.	2 hr.[8]	<20' fm. p/l 1 3/4 hr., N.A. <5' fm. p/l [1803b]	4 hr.	1 hr.	2 hr.
II F.R.	29,900	44,850	59,800	59,800	1 story × 3, >1 story × 2	4 stories 160'	4 hr.	2 hr.	"	2 hr.	1 hr.	2 hr.	2 hr.	1 hr.[8]	" [1903b]	4 hr.	1 hr.	2 hr.
	13,500	20,250	27,000	27,000	"	2 stories 65'	1 hr., <10' fm. p/l 2 hr. [5A]	1 hr.	1 hr., <10' fm. p/l N.A. <5' fm. p/l 2 hr.[6] [5A]	1 hr.	1 hr.	1 hr.	1 hr.	1 hr.[8, 9]	<10' fm. p/l 1 3/4 hr., N.A. <5' fm. p/l [5A]	2 hr.	1 hr.	1 hr., ≥4 stories 2 hr.
	13,500	20,250	27,000	27,000	"	2 stories 65'	4 hr.	1 hr.	1 hr., <20' fm. p/l 2 hr. <5' fm. p/l 4 hr.[6] [5A]	1 hr.	1 hr.	1 hr.	1 hr.	1 hr.[9]	<20' fm. p/l 1 3/4 hr., N.A. <5' fm. p/l [2003b]	4 hr.	1 hr.	"
	13,500	20,250	27,000	27,000	"	2 stories 65'	4 hr.	1 hr.	"	1 hr. or H.T.	1 hr. or H.T.	1 hr.	H.T.	H.T.	" [2103b]	4 hr.	1 hr.	"

A. **Each Page:** represents a single occupancy group.
B. **Each Row:** represents each construction type allowed for the occupancy.
C. **Each Page:** represents the building square footage, building height, and construction requirements for one occupancy.
D. **Each Column:** coordinates with a checklist item.

E. **"Figures" or Answers:** are given within each table box.
F. **Footnotes:** may be given for further explanation or exceptions and are listed with each table.
G. **UBC Reference Numbers:** are given for all table information, for any further research desired at a later phase.
H. **Abbreviations and Symbols:** are listed on page ix.

PROJECT:_____

DATE:_____

RESEARCHER:_____

Occupancy:_____

Construction type:_____

	INFORMATION	REFERENCE	NOTES
SQUARE FOOTAGE			
Max. sq. ft.			
2 yards ≥ 20' wide			
3 yards ≥ 20' wide			
All yards ≥ 20' wide			
Addit. sq. ft. if sprinklered			
BUILDING HEIGHT			
Maximum ft.			
Maximum stories			
CONSTRUCTION			
Exterior bearing walls			
Interior bearing walls			
Exterior non-bearing walls			
Interior non-bearing walls			
Structural frame			
Permanent partitions			
Shaft enclosures			
Floors/ceilings			
Roofs/ceilings			
Exterior doors and windows			
Area separation walls			

Code Research Checklist

PROJECT:_____

DATE:_____

RESEARCHER:_____

Occupancy:_____

Construction type:_____

	INFORMATION		REFERENCE	NOTES
CONSTRUCTION (cont.)				
Exit corridors				
Exit stairways				
LIGHT, VENTILATION, SANITATION				
Min. facilities required	STANDARD	BARRIER-FREE		
Water closets				
Urinals				
Lavatories				
Drinking fountains				
EXITING				
Occupant load				
Use #1				
Area				
Occupant load factor				
Occupant load				
Use #2				
Area				
Occupant load factor				
Occupant load				
Use #3				
Area				

BUILDING CODE QUICK REFERENCE GUIDE
PROFESSIONAL PUBLICATIONS, INC.

PROJECT:_____

DATE:_____

RESEARCHER:_____

Occupancy:_____

Construction type:_____

	INFORMATION			REFERENCE	NOTES
EXITING (cont.)					
Occupant load factor					
Occupant load					
Total occupant load					
Number of exits required					
Minimum exit width					
Minimum stair width, maximum stair rise, and minimum stair run	WIDTH	RISE	RUN		
Minimum corridor width					
Minimum corridor height					
Maximum distance to exits					
If building is sprinklered					
If last portion of exit is w/in 1-hr. corridor					
Exit door minimum width					
Exit door minimum height					
Horizontal exit use					
# of occupants served					
Discharge area sq. ft. required					

Code Research Checklist

PROJECT:_____

DATE:_____

RESEARCHER:_____

Occupancy:_____

Construction type:_____

	INFORMATION			REFERENCE	NOTES
EXITING (cont.)					
Smokeproof enclosures					
Required if building has occupied floors higher than					
Construction	WALLS	FLR/CLG	OPENINGS		
Minimum vestibule size					
Exit court use					
# of occupants served					
Court width required					
Construction	WALLS	OPENINGS			
Exit passageway use Construction	WALLS/FLR/CLG	OPENINGS			
LOCAL GOVERNING AGENCY'S REQUIREMENTS					
(city/county/state) Zoning					
Setbacks required					
Front yard					
Side yard					
Back yard					
Bulk plane(s) (if applicable)					

PROJECT:_____

DATE:_____

RESEARCHER:_____

Occupancy:_____

Construction type:_____

	INFORMATION	REFERENCE	NOTES
LOCAL GOVERNING AGENCY'S REQUIREMENTS (city/county/state) (cont.)			
Maximum building height			
Parking required			
Standard spaces			
Ratio of compact spaces allowed			
Ratio/number of barrier-free spaces required			
Floor area ratio (F.A.R.) allowed (if applicable)			
Percent of site landscaping required (if applicable)			

Occupancy Descriptions

Table OD.1 **Occupancy Descriptions [5A]**

Group	Description
A-1	Assembly w/stage & an occ. load ≥1,000
A-2	Assembly w/stage & an occ. load <1,000
A-2.1	Assembly w/out a stage & an occ. load ≥300
A-3	Assembly w/out a stage & an occ. load <300
B-1	Repair garages w/no open flame or hazardous materials
B-2	Bars w/an occ. load <50
	Educational facilities for students beyond the 12th grade w/an occ. load <50
	Factories
	Fire stations
	Office buildings
	Paint stores w/out bulk handling
	Police stations
	Print shops/plants
	Restaurants w/an occ. load <50
	Retail stores
	Storage & salesrooms for combustible goods
	Wholesale stores
B-3	Aircraft hangars w/no open flame or welding
	Helistops
	Open parking garages
B-4	Cold storage
	Creameries
	Factories w/non-combusts. & non-explosives
	Ice plants
	Power plants
	Pumping plants
	Storage & salesrooms of non-combustibles

Group	Description
E-1	Educational up to 12th grade with ≥50 occ.
E-2	Educational up to 12th grade with <50 occ.
E-3	Day care with >6 occ.
H (ALL)	Hazardous (see H occupancy definitions)
I-1.1	Hospitals
	Nurseries with >5 children <6 years old
	Nursing homes & sanitariums for non-ambulatory persons
I-1.2	Health care buildings for >5 ambulatory persons
I-2	Nursing homes for >5 ambulatory persons
I-3	Jails
	Mental hospitals
	Prisons
	Reformatories
R-1	Apartments with >10 residents
	Congregate residences with >10 residents
	Lodging houses with >10 residents
R-3	Congregate residences with ≤10 residents
	Dwellings
	Lodging houses with ≤10 residents
R-4	Residential group care facilities for >5 but ≤18 ambulatory, non-restrained residents (excluding staff)

Table CT.1 **Construction Type General Descriptions**

Construction Type	Structural Elements	Walls	Square Feet	Building Height/Stories	Relative Expense
I	Steel	Non-combustible	Usually	Usually	High
	Concrete	Fire-resistive	Unlimited[1]	Unlimited[2]	
	Masonry				
II					
	Masonry	Non-combustible	II F.R.-high	II F.R.-high	Average-high
			II-1-hr.-average	II-1-hr.-average	
			II N-average	II N-average	
III	Any	Non-combustible[3]	Average	Average	Low-average
IV (Heavy-Timber)	Any	Non-combustible	Average	Low-average	Average-high
V	Any	Any (some restrictions)	Low-average	Low	Low-average

1. Except in H-1, H-2, and R-4 occupancies.

2. Except in H-1, H-2, H-6, H-7, and R-4 occupancies.

3. Type III buildings usually have high fire-resistive requirements for exterior walls, low fire-resistive requirements for structural frame and interior walls.

Part 1

Building Occupancies

1

A Occupancies

Table 1.1 A-1 Assembly Occupancy

A-1	MAXIMUM ALLOWABLE SQ. FT.						CONSTRUCTION (FIRE-RESISTIVE REQUIREMENTS IN HOURS)											
	For 1 Story Buildings[1] [5C]	2 Side Yards >20' Add 1¼% Per Foot Over 20'[2] [506a]	3 Side Yards >20' Add 2½% Per Foot Over 20'[2] [506a]	All Side Yards >20' Add 5% Per Foot Over 20'[2] [506a]	Additional Sq. Ft. If Sprinklered[3] [506c]	Maximum Building Height[4] [5D,507]	Exterior Bearing Walls [17A]	Interior Bearing Walls [17A]	Exterior Non-bearing Walls	Structural Frame [17A]	Permanent Partitions [17A]	Shaft Enclosures [17A]	Floors/ Ceilings [17A]	Roofs/ Ceilings [17A]	Exterior Doors & Windows	Area Separation Walls[7] [505f]	Exit Corridors [3305g]	Exit Stairways [3306l]
Type I	Unlimited	Unlimited	Unlimited	Unlimited	Unlimited	Unlimited	4 hr.	3 hr.	1 hr., <20' fm. p/l 2 hr., <5' fm. p/l 4 hr.[5]	3 hr.	1 hr.	2 hr.	2 hr.	2 hr.[6]	<20' fm. p/l 3/4 hr., N.A. <5' fm. p/l [1803b]	4 hr.	1 hr.	2 hr.
II F.R.	29,000	44,850	59,800	59,800	1 story × 3, >1 story × 2	4 stories 160'	4 hr.	2 hr.	"	2 hr.	1 hr.	2 hr.	2 hr.	1 hr.[6]	" [1903b]	4 hr.	1 hr.	2 hr.

1. The total combined area for multistory buildings may be 2× that shown, and the area of any single story must be ≤ that given above. **Figures given are maximums.** [505]

2. The maximum floor areas given "FOR 1 STORY BUILDINGS" may be increased where public ways or yards are ≥20' wide, according to the **rates** given here. **Figures given are maximums.** [506a]

3. The multiplying factor given here (a doubling or tripling of allowed sq. ft.) shall not apply when sprinklers are used to: increase the number of stories; substitute for 1-hr. const.; include atria; or use in an H-1, H-2, H-3, or H-7 occupancy. [506c]

4. These story limits may be increased by one story if the building is fully sprinklered, provided no other increase for sprinkling is used. [507]

5. Non-bearing walls fronting public ways or yards ≥40' wide may be non-rated, non-combust. [1803a, 1903a, 2003a, 2103a]

6. a. Roof const., including struct. frame, >25' above all floors/levels in A or E type I, II-F.R., or II-1-hr. or an atrium, may be non-rated.

   b. Ceilings in A or E type I, II-F.R., or II-1-hr. >18' but <25' above all floors/levels may be only 1-hr. [1806]

7. See Chapter 7, "Area Separations," page 80.

Table 1.2 A-2 and A-2.1 Assembly Occupancies

A-2 & A-2.1	MAXIMUM ALLOWABLE SQ. FT.					Maximum Building Height[4] [5D,507]	CONSTRUCTION (FIRE-RESISTIVE REQUIREMENTS IN HOURS)											
	For 1 Story Buildings[1] [5C]	2 Side Yards >20' Add 1 1/4% Per Foot Over 20'[2] [506a]	3 Side Yards >20' Add 2 1/2% Per Foot Over 20'[2] [506a]	All Side Yards >20' Add 5% Per Foot Over 20'[2] [506a]	Additional Sq. Ft. If Sprinklered[3] [506c]		Exterior Bearing Walls [17A]	Interior Bearing Walls [17A]	Exterior Non-bearing Walls	Structural Frame [17A]	Permanent Partitions [17A]	Shaft Enclosures [17A]	Floors/ Ceilings [17A]	Roofs/ Ceilings [17A]	Exterior Doors & Windows	Area Separation Walls[10] [505f]	Exit Corridors [3305g]	Exit Stairways [3306l]
Type I	Unlimited	Unlimited	Unlimited	Unlimited	Unlimited	Unlimited	4 hr.	3 hr.	1 hr., <20' fm. p/l 2 hr., <5' fm. p/l 4 hr.[6]	3 hr.	1 hr.	2 hr.	2 hr.	2 hr.[8]	<20' fm. p/l 3/4 hr., N.A. <5' fm. p/l [1803b]	4 hr.	1 hr.	2 hr.
II F.R.	29,000	44,850	59,800	59,800	1 story × 3, >1 story × 2	4 stories 160'	4 hr.	2 hr.	"	2 hr.	1 hr.	2 hr.	2 hr.	1 hr.[8]	" [1903b]	4 hr.	1 hr.	2 hr.
II 1-HR	13,500	20,250	27,000	27,000	"	2 stories 65'	1 hr., <10' fm. p/l 2 hr. [5A]	1 hr.	1 hr., <10' fm. p/l 2 hr.[6] [5A]	1 hr.	1 hr.	1 hr.	1 hr.	1 hr.[8, 9]	<10' fm. p/l 3/4 hr., N.A. <5' fm. p/l [5A]	2 hr.	1 hr.	1 hr., ≥ 4 stories 2 hr.
III 1-HR	13,500	20,250	27,000	27,000	"	2 stories 65'	4 hr.	1 hr.	1 hr., <20' fm. p/l 2 hr., <5' fm. p/l 4 hr.[6]	1 hr.	1 hr.	1 hr.	1 hr.	1 hr.[9]	<20' fm. p/l 3/4 hr., N.A. <5' fm. p/l [2003b]	4 hr.	1 hr.	"
IV H.T.	13,500	20,250	27,000	27,000	"	2 stories 65'	4 hr.	1 hr.	"	1 hr. or H.T.	1 hr. or H.T.	1 hr.	H.T.	H.T.	" [2103b]	4 hr.	1 hr.	"
V 1-HR[4]	10,500	15,750	21,000	21,000	"	2 stories 50'	1 hr., <10' fm. p/l 2 hr. [5A]	1 hr.	1 hr., <10' fm. p/l 2 hr.[6]	1 hr.	1 hr.	1 hr.[7]	1 hr.	1 hr.[9]	<10' fm. p/l 3/4 hr., N.A. <5' fm. p/l [5A]	2 hr.	1 hr.	"

1. The total combined area for multistory buildings may be 2× that shown, and the area of any single story must be ≤ that given above. **Figures given are maximums**. [505]

2. The maximum floor areas given "FOR 1 STORY BUILDINGS" may be increased where public ways or yards are ≥20' wide, according to the **rates** given here. **Figures given are maximums.** [506a]

3. The multiplying factor given here (a doubling or tripling of allowed sq. ft.) shall not apply when sprinklers are used to: increase the number of stories; substitute for 1-hr. const.; include atria; or use in an H-1, H-2, H-3, or H-7 occupancy. [506c]

4. These story limits may be increased by one story if the building is fully sprinklered, provided no other increase for sprinkling is used. [507]

5. A-2.1 type V-1-hr. only allowed if occupant load is <1,000. [602c]

6. Non-bearing walls fronting public ways or yards ≥40' wide may be non-rated, non-combust. [1803a, 1903a, 2003a, 2103a]

7. Rated shafts are not required for:

   a. Openings between one floor only, not concealed w/in building const.

   b. In type V buildings, chutes and dumbwaiters <9 sq. ft. in cross-sectional area and lined w/gyp. bd. and sheet metal.

   c. Gas vents, factory-built chimneys, and piping through two floors max. [1706]

8. a. Roof const., including struct. frame, >25' above all floors/levels in A or E type I, II-F.R., or II-1-hr. or an atrium, may be non-rated.

   b. Ceilings in A or E type I, II-F.R., or II-1-hr. >18' but <25' above all floors/levels may be only 1-hr. [1806]

   c. Roof const., in A-2.1 occupancies of type I, II-F.R., or II-1-hr. with an occupant load ≥10,000, <25' above all floors/levels may be non-rated if:

   1. the building is only one story,

   and

   2. the building is sprinklered,

   and

   3. the area lower than 25' is <35 percent of the entire building floor area. [1806]

9. A fire-resistive ceiling may be omitted in one-story buildings if the roof framing is completely open to the room. [602]

10. See Chapter 7, "Area Separations," page 80.

Table 1.3   **A-3 Assembly Occupancy**

A-3	MAXIMUM ALLOWABLE SQ. FT.					Maximum Building Height [4] [5D,507]	CONSTRUCTION (FIRE-RESISTIVE REQUIREMENTS IN HOURS)											
	For 1 Story Buildings[1] [5C]	2 Side Yards >20' Add 1¼% Per Foot Over 20'[2] [506a]	3 Side Yards >20' Add 2½% Per Foot Over 20'[2] [506a]	All Side Yards >20' Add 5% Per Foot Over 20'[2] [506a]	Additional Sq. Ft. If Sprinklered[3] [506c]		Exterior Bearing Walls [17A]	Interior Bearing Walls [17A]	Exterior Non-bearing Walls	Structural Frame [17A]	Permanent Partitions [17A]	Shaft Enclosures [17A]	Floors/ Ceilings [17A]	Roofs/ Ceilings [17A]	Exterior Doors & Windows	Area Separation Walls[10] [505f]	Exit Corridors [3305g]	Exit Stairways [3306l]
Type I	Unlimited	Unlimited	Unlimited	Unlimited	Unlimited	Unlimited	4 hr.	3 hr.	1 hr., <10' fm. p/l 2 hr., <5' fm. p/l 4 hr.[5]	3 hr.	1 hr.	2 hr.	2 hr.	2 hr.[7]	<20' fm. p/l 1¾ hr., N.A. <5' fm. p/l [1803b]	4 hr.	1 hr.	2 hr.
II F.R.	29,000	44,850	59,800	59,800	1 story × 3, >1 story × 2	12 stories 160'	4 hr.	2 hr.	"	2 hr.	1 hr.	2 hr.	2 hr.	1 hr.[7]	" [1903b]	4 hr.	1 hr.	2 hr.
II 1-HR	13,500	20,250	27,000	27,000	"	2 stories 65'	1 hr., <5' fm. p/l 2 hr. [5A]	1 hr.	1 hr., <5' fm. p/l 2 hr. [5A][5]	1 hr.	1 hr.	1 hr.	1 hr.	1 hr.[7,8]	<10' fm. p/l 1¾ hr., N.A. <5' fm. p/l [5A]	2 hr.	1 hr.	1 hr., ≥4 stories 2 hr.
II N	9,100	13,650	18,200	18,200	"	1 story 55'	None, <20' fm. p/l 1 hr., <5' fm. p/l 2 hr. [5A]	None	None, <20' fm. p/l 1 hr., <5' fm. p/l 2 hr.[5] [5A]	None	None	1 hr.	None	None	" [5A]	2 hr.	1 hr.[10]	"
III 1-HR	13,500	20,250	27,000	27,000	"	2 stories 65'	4 hr.	1 hr.	1 hr., <10' fm. p/l 2 hr., <5' fm. p/l 4 hr.[5]	1 hr.	1 hr.	1 hr.	1 hr.	1 hr.[8]	<20' fm. p/l 1¾ hr., N.A. <5' fm. p/l [2003b]	4 hr.	1 hr.	"
III N	9,100	13,650	18,200	18,200	"	1 story 55'	4 hr.	None	"	None	None	1 hr.	None	None	" [2003b]	4 hr.	1 hr.[10]	"
IV H.T.	13,500	20,250	27,000	27,000	"	2 stories 65'	4 hr.	1 hr.	"	1 hr. or H.T.	1 hr. or H.T.	1 hr.	H.T.	H.T.	" [2103b]	4 hr.	1 hr.	"
V 1-HR	10,500	15,750	21,000	21,000	"	2 stories 50'	1 hr., <5' fm. p/l 2 hr. [5A]	1 hr.	1 hr., <5' fm. p/l 2 hr. [5A]	1 hr.	1 hr.	1 hr.[6]	1 hr.	1 hr.[8]	<10' fm. p/l 1¾ hr., N.A. <5' fm. p/l [5A]	2 hr.	1 hr.	"
V N	6,000	9,000	12,000	12,000	"	1 story 40'	None, <20' fm. p/l 1 hr., <5' fm. p/l 2 hr. [5A]	None	None, <20' fm. p/l 1 hr., <5' fm. p/l 2 hr. [5A]	None	None	1 hr.[6]	None	None	" [5A]	2 hr.	1 hr.[10]	"

1. The total combined area for multistory buildings may be 2× that shown, and the area of any single story must be ≤ that given above. **Figures given are maximums.** [505]

2. The maximum floor areas given "FOR 1 STORY BUILDINGS" may be increased where public ways or yards are ≥20' wide, according to the **rates** given here. **Figures given are maximums.** [506a]

3. The multiplying factor given here (a doubling or tripling of allowed sq. ft.) shall not apply when sprinklers are used to: increase the number of stories; substitute for 1-hr. const.; include atria; or use in an H-1, H-2, H-3, or H-7 occupancy. [506c]

4. These story limits may be increased by one story if the building is fully sprinklered, provided no other increase for sprinkling is used. [507]

5. Non-bearing walls fronting public ways or yards ≥40' wide may be non-rated, non-combust. [1803a, 1903a, 2003a, 2103a]

6. Rated shafts are not required for:

   a. Openings between one floor only, not concealed w/in building const.

   b. In type V buildings, chutes and dumbwaiters <9 sq. ft. in cross-sectional area and lined w/gyp. bd. and sheet metal.

   c. Gas vents, factory-built chimneys and piping through 2 floors max. [1706]

7. a. Roof const., including struct. frame, >25' above all floors/levels in A or E type I, II-F.R., or II-1-hr. or an atrium, may be non-rated.

   b. Ceilings in A or E type I, II-F.R., or II-1-hr. >18' but <25' above all floors/levels may be only 1-hr. [1806]

8. A fire-resistive ceiling may be omitted in one-story buildings if the roof framing is completely open to the room. [602]

9. See Chapter 7, "Area Separations" page 80.

10. Corridors in non-rated buildings serving an occupant load <30 may be non-rated (excluding R-1 or any I occupancy). [3305g]

Table 1.4 A-4 Assembly Occupancy

A-4	MAXIMUM ALLOWABLE SQ. FT.					Maximum Building Height [4] [5D,507]	CONSTRUCTION (FIRE-RESISTIVE REQUIREMENTS IN HOURS)											
	For 1 Story Buildings[1] [5C]	2 Side Yards >20' Add 1 1/4% Per Foot Over 20' [2] [506a]	3 Side Yards >20' Add 2 1/2% Per Foot Over 20' [2] [506a]	All Side Yards >20' Add 5% Per Foot Over 20' [2] [506a]	Additional Sq. Ft. If Sprinklered [3] [506c]		Exterior Bearing Walls [17A]	Interior Bearing Walls [17A]	Exterior Non-bearing Walls	Structural Frame [17A]	Permanent Partitions [17A]	Shaft Enclosures [17A]	Floors/ Ceilings [17A]	Roofs/ Ceilings [17A]	Exterior Doors & Windows	Area Separation Walls [10] [505f]	Exit Corridors [3305g]	Exit Stairways [3306I]
Type I	Unlimited	Unlimited	Unlimited	Unlimited	Unlimited	Unlimited	4 hr.	3 hr.	1 hr., <10' fm. p/l 2 hr.[5]	3 hr.	1 hr.	2 hr.	2 hr.	2 hr. [7]	<20' fm. p/l 3/4 hr. [1803b]	4 hr.	1 hr.	2 hr.
II F.R.	29,000[11]	44,850	59,800	59,800	1 story × 3, >1 story × 2	12 stories 160'	4 hr.	2 hr.	"	2 hr.	1 hr.	2 hr.	2 hr.	1 hr. [7]	" [1903b]	4 hr.	1 hr.	2 hr.
II 1-HR	13,500[11]	20,250	27,000	27,000	"	2 stories 65'	1 hr. [5A]	1 hr.	1 hr.[5] [5A]	1 hr.	1 hr.	1 hr.	1 hr.	1 hr.[7, 8]	<10' fm. p/l 3/4 hr. [5A]	2 hr.	1 hr.	1 hr., ≥ 4 stories 2 hr.
II N	9,100[11]	13,650	18,200	18,200	"	1 story 55'	None, <10' fm. p/l 1 hr. [5A]	None	None, <10' fm. p/l 1 hr.[5] [5A]	None	None	1 hr.	None	None	" [5A]	2 hr.	1 hr.[10]	"
III 1-HR	13,500[11]	20,250	27,000	27,000	"	2 stories 65'	4 hr.	1 hr.	1 hr., <10' fm. p/l 2 hr. [5]	1 hr.	1 hr.	1 hr.	1 hr.	1 hr.[8]	<20' fm. p/l 3/4 hr. [2003b]	4 hr.	1 hr.	"
III N	9,100[11]	13,650	18,200	18,200	"	1 story 55'	4 hr.	None	"	None	None	1 hr.	None	None	" [2003b]	4 hr.	1 hr.[10]	"
IV H.T.	13,500[11]	20,250	27,000	27,000	"	2 stories 65'	4 hr.	1 hr.	"	1 hr. or H.T.	1 hr. or H.T.	1 hr.	H.T.	H.T.	" [2103b]	4 hr.	1 hr.	"
V 1-HR	10,500[11]	15,750	21,000	21,000	"	2 stories 50'	1 hr.[5A]	1 hr.	1 hr. [5A]	1 hr.	1 hr.	1 hr.[6]	1 hr.	1 hr.[8]	<10' fm. p/l 3/4 hr. [5A]	2 hr.	1 hr.	"
V N	6,000[11]	9,000	12,000	12,000	"	1 story 40'	None, <10' fm. p/l	None	None, <10' fm. p/l 1 hr. [5A]	None	None	1 hr.[6]	None	None	" [5A]	2 hr.	1 hr.[10]	"

1. The total combined area for multistory buildings may be 2× that shown, and the area of any single story must be ≤ that given above. **Figures given are maximums.** [505]

2. The maximum floor areas given "FOR 1 STORY BUILDINGS" may be increased where public ways or yards are ≥20' wide, according to the **rates** given here. **Figures given are maximums.** [506a]

3. The multiplying factor given here (a doubling or tripling of allowed sq. ft.) shall not apply when sprinklers are used to: increase the number of stories; substitute for 1-hr. const.; include atria; or use in an H-1, H-2, H-3, or H-7 occupancy. [506c]

4. These story limits may be increased by one story if the building is fully sprinklered, provided no other increase for sprinkling is used. [507]

5. Non-bearing walls fronting public ways or yards ≥40' wide may be non-rated, non-combust. [1803a, 1903a, 2003a, 2103a]

6. Rated shafts are not required for:

   a. Openings between one floor only, not concealed w/in building const.

   b. In type V buildings, chutes and dumbwaiters <9 sq. ft. in cross-sectional area and lined w/gyp. bd. and sheet metal.

   c. Gas vents, factory-built chimneys, and piping through two floors max. [1706]

7. a. Roof const., including struct. frame, >25' above all floors/levels in A or E type I, II-F.R., or II-1-hr. or an atrium, may be non-rated.

   b. Ceilings in A or E type I, II-F.R., or II-1-hr. >18' but <25' above all floors/levels may be only 1-hr. [1806]

8. A fire-resistive ceiling may be omitted in one-story buildings if the roof framing is completely open to the room. [602]

9. See Chapter 7, "Area Separations," page 80.

10. Corridors in non-rated buildings serving an occupant load <30 may be non-rated (excluding R-1 or any I occupancy). [3305g]

11. Excluding grandstands, bleachers, and open reviewing stands. [601]

General Sanitation [510]

Water closet rooms: Must be separated from food preparation/storage areas by a tight-fitting door.

Floors and walls in water closets rooms and showers: Must be of smooth, non-absorbent, hard finishes w/ a min. 5" base.

Walls must be so finished up to a minimum 48".

Shower walls must be so finished up to a minimum 7".

Light [605]

All occupied rooms must have either: Window opening(s) $\geq$ $^1/_{10}$ the floor area of the room.

or

Artificial light.

Ventilation [605]

All occupied rooms must have either: Openable window(s) with an area $\geq$$^1/_{20}$ the floor area of the room.

or

Mechanical ventilation.

Toilet Rooms [605]

Toilet rooms must have ventilation by either: Openable window(s) $\geq$ 3 sq. ft.

or

Mechanical ventilation.

At least one lavatory for every two water closets for each sex must be provided.

Barrier-free access: $\geq$1 of each sanitary fixture provided per floor must be accessible.

UPC recommended:

Employee Use (fixtures:persons)

Water Closets	Urinals	Lavs
1:1–15	1:50	1:40
2:16–35		
3:36–55		
>55 persons, add 1:40 persons		

Public Use

Water Closets		Urinals	Lavs
Male	*Female*		
1:1–100	3:1–100	1:1–100	1:1–200
2:101–200	6:101–200	2:101–200	2:201–400
3:201–400	8:201–400	3:201–400	3:401–750
>400 persons, add 1:500 males and 1:300 females		4:401–600 >600, add 1:300 males	>750 add 1:500 persons

Drinking Fountains [605]

At least one drinking fountain per floor must be provided.

Barrier-free access: $\geq$1 fountain per floor must be accessible to those in wheelchairs, and $\geq$1 fountain per floor must be accessible to those who have difficulty bending.

UPC recommended: 1:75 persons.

2

B Occupancies

Table 2.1   **B-1 and B-2 Commercial Occupancies**

B-1 & B-2	MAXIMUM ALLOWABLE SQ. FT.					Maximum Building Height[4] [5D,507]	CONSTRUCTION (FIRE-RESISTIVE REQUIREMENTS IN HOURS)											
	For 1 Story Buildings[1] [5C]	2 Side Yards >20' Add 1¼% Per Foot Over 20'[2] [506a]	3 Side Yards >20' Add 2½% Per Foot Over 20'[2] [506a]	All Side Yards >20' Add 5% Per Foot Over 20'[2] [506a]	Additional Sq. Ft. If Sprinklered[3] [506c]		Exterior Bearing Walls [17A]	Interior Bearing Walls [17A]	Exterior Non-bearing Walls	Structural Frame [17A]	Permanent Partitions [17A]	Shaft Enclosures [17A]	Floors/ Ceilings [17A]	Roofs/ Ceilings [17A]	Exterior Doors & Windows	Area Separation Walls[10] [505f]	Exit Corridors [3305g]	Exit Stairways [3306l]
Type I	Unlimited	Unlimited	Unlimited	Unlimited	Unlimited	Unlimited	2 hr., <5' fm. p/l 4 hr.	3 hr.	1 hr., <10' fm. p/l 2 hr., <5' fm. p/l 4 hr.[5]	3 hr.	1 hr.	2 hr.	2 hr.	2 hr.[11]	<20' fm. p/l 1¾ hr., N.A. <5' fm. p/l [1803b]	4 hr.	1 hr.	2 hr.
II F.R.	39,900	59,850	79,800	79,800	1 story × 3, >2 story × 2[9]	12 stories 160'	"	2 hr.	"	2 hr.	1 hr.	2 hr.	2 hr.	1 hr.[11]	" [1903b]	4 hr.	1 hr.	2 hr.
II 1-HR	18,000	27,000	36,000	36,000	"	4 stories 65'	1 hr. [5A]	1 hr.	1 hr.[5] [5A]	1 hr.	1 hr.	1 hr.	1 hr.	1 hr.[11]	<10' fm. p/l 1¾ hr., N.A. <5' fm. p/l [5A]	2 hr.	1 hr.	1 hr., ≥ 4 stories 2 hr.
II N	12,000	18,000	24,000	24,000	"	2 stories 55'	None, <20' fm. p/l 1 hr. [5A]	None	None, <20' fm. p/l 1 hr.[5] [5A]	None	None	1 hr.	None	None	"	2 hr.	1 hr.[8]	"
III 1-HR	18,000	27,000	36,000	36,000	"	4 stories 65'	2 hr., <5' fm. p/l 4 hr.	1 hr.	1 hr., <10' fm. p/l 2 hr., <5' fm. p/l 4 hr.[5]	1 hr.	1 hr.	1 hr.	1 hr.	1 hr.	<20' fm. p/l 1¾ hr., N.A. <5' fm. p/l [2003b]	4 hr.	1 hr.	"
III N	12,000	18,000	24,000	24,000	"	2 stories 55'	"	None	"	None	None	1 hr.	None	None	"	4 hr.	1 hr.[8]	"
IV H.T.	18,000	27,000	36,000	36,000	"	4 stories 65'	"	1 hr.	"	1 hr. or H.T.	1 hr. or H.T.	1 hr.	H.T.	H.T.	" [2103b]	4 hr.	1 hr.	"
V 1-HR	14,000	21,000	28,000	28,000	"	3 stories 50'	1 hr. [5A]	1 hr.	1 hr. [5A]	1 hr.	1 hr.	1 hr.[6]	1 hr.	1 hr.	<10' fm. p/l 1¾ hr., N.A. <5' fm. p/l [5A]	2 hr.	1 hr.	"
V N	8,000	12,000	16,000	16,000	"	2 stories 40'	None, <20' fm. p/l 1 hr. [5A]	None	None, <20' fm. p/l 1 hr. [5A]	None	None	1 hr.[6]	None	None	"	2 hr.	1 hr.[8]	"

1. The total combined area for multistory buildings may be 2× that shown, and the area of any single story must be ≤ that given above. **Figures given are maximums.** [505]

2. The maximum floor areas given "FOR 1 STORY BUILDINGS" may be increased where public ways or yards are ≥20' wide, according to the **rates** given here. **Figures given are maximums.** [506a]

3. The multiplying factor given here (a doubling or tripling of allowed sq. ft.) shall not apply when sprinklers are used to: increase the number of stories; substitute for 1-hr. const.; include atria; or use in an H-1, H-2, H-3, or H-7 occupancy. [506c]

4. These story limits may be increased by one story if the building is fully sprinklered, provided no other increase for sprinkling is used. [507]

5. Non-bearing walls fronting public ways or yards ≥40' wide may be non-rated, non-combust. [1803a, 1903a, 2003a, 2103a]

6. Rated shafts are not required for:

   a. Openings between 1 floor only, not concealed w/in building const.

   b. In type V buildings, chutes and dumbwaiters <9 sq. ft. in cross-sectional area and lined w/gyp. bd. and sheet metal.

   c. Gas vents, factory-built chimneys, and piping through two floors max.

   d. Sprinkled B occupancies need not enclose escalators that have draft curtains. [1706]

7. See Chapter 7, "Area Separations," section, page 80.

8. Corridors in non-rated buildings serving an occupant load <30 may be non-rated (excluding R-1 or any I occupancy). [3305g]

9. The area of any one- or two-story B or H-5 fully-sprinklered building with all yards ≥60' wide may be unlimited. [506b]

10. Corridors w/in office spaces with ≤100 occupants may be non-rated. [3305g]

11. Roof const. (other than primary members) in type I, II-F.R., or II-1-hr. ≥25' above all floors/levels may be non-rated, non-combust. H.T. const. may be used if such building is only one story. [1806]

Table 2.2 B-3 Commercial Occupancy

B-3	MAXIMUM ALLOWABLE SQ. FT.					Maximum Building Height[4] [5D,507]	CONSTRUCTION (FIRE-RESISTIVE REQUIREMENTS IN HOURS)											
	For 1 Story Buildings[1] [5C]	2 Side Yards >20' Add 1¼% Per Foot Over 20'[2] [506a]	3 Side Yards >20' Add 2½% Per Foot Over 20'[2] [506a]	All Side Yards >20' Add 5% Per Foot Over 20'[2] [506a]	Additional Sq. Ft. If Sprinklered[3] [506c]		Exterior Bearing Walls [17A]	Interior Bearing Walls [17A]	Exterior Non-bearing Walls [17A]	Structural Frame [17A]	Permanent Partitions [17A]	Shaft Enclosures [17A]	Floors/Ceilings [17A]	Roofs/Ceilings [17A]	Exterior Doors & Windows	Area Separation Walls[7] [505f]	Exit Corridors [3305g]	Exit Stairways [3306l]
Type I	Unlimited	Unlimited	Unlimited	Unlimited	Unlimited	Unlimited	2 hr., <5' fm. p/l 4 hr.	3 hr.	1 hr., <20' fm. p/l 2 hr., <5' fm. p/l 4 hr.[5]	3 hr.	1 hr.	2 hr.	2 hr.	2 hr.[10]	<20' fm. p/l 1¾ hr., N.A. <5' fm. p/l [1803b]	4 hr.	1 hr.	2 hr.
II F.R.	39,900	59,850	79,800	79,800	1 & 2 stories × 3, >2 story × 2[9]	12 stories 160'	"	2 hr.	"	2 hr.	1 hr.	2 hr.	2 hr.	1 hr.[10]	" [1903b]	4 hr.	1 hr.	2 hr.
II 1-HR	18,000	27,000	36,000	36,000	"	4 stories 65'	1 hr. [5A]	1 hr.	1 hr.[5] [5A]	1 hr.	1 hr.	1 hr.	1 hr.	1 hr.[10]	<20' fm. p/l 1¾ hr., N.A. <5' fm. p/l [5A]	2 hr.	1 hr.	1 hr., ≥ 4 stories 2 hr.
II N	12,000	18,000	24,000	24,000	"	2 stories 55'	None, <20' fm. p/l 1 hr. [5A]	None	None, <20' fm. p/l 1 hr.[5] [5A]	None	None	1 hr.	None	None	"	2 hr.	1 hr.[8]	"
III 1-HR	18,000	27,000	36,000	36,000	"	4 stories 65'	2 hr., <5' fm. p/l 4 hr.	1 hr.	1 hr., <20' fm. p/l 2 hr., <5' fm. p/l 4 hr.[5]	1 hr.	1 hr.	1 hr.	1 hr.	1 hr.	<20' fm. p/l 1¾ hr., N.A. <5' fm. p/l [2003b]	4 hr.	1 hr.	"
III N	12,000	18,000	24,000	24,000	"	2 stories 55'	"	None	"	None	None	1 hr.	None	None	"	4 hr.	1 hr.[8]	"
IV H.T.	18,000	27,000	36,000	36,000	"	4 stories 65'	"	1 hr.	"	1 hr. or H.T.	1 hr. or H.T.	1 hr.	H.T.	H.T.	" [2103b]	4 hr.	1 hr.	"
V 1-HR	14,000	21,000	28,000	28,000	"	3 stories 50'	1 hr. [5A]	1 hr.	1 hr. [5A]	1 hr.	1 hr.	1 hr.[6]	1 hr.	1 hr.	<20' fm. p/l 1¾ hr., N.A. <5' fm. p/l [5A]	2 hr.	1 hr.	"
V N	8,000	12,000	16,000	16,000	"	2 stories 40'	None, <20' fm. p/l 1 hr. [5A]	None	None, <20' fm. p/l 1 hr. [5A]	None	None	1 hr.[6]	None	None	"	2 hr.	1 hr.[8]	"

Note: For open parking garages, see page 30.

1. The total combined area for multistory buildings may be 2× that shown, and the area of any single story must be ≤ that given above. **Figures given are maximums.** [505]

2. The maximum floor areas given "FOR 1 STORY BUILDINGS" may be increased where public ways or yards are ≥20' wide, according to the **rates** given here. **Figures given are maximums.** [506a]

3. The multiplying factor given here (a doubling or tripling of allowed sq. ft.) shall not apply when sprinklers are used to: increase the number of stories; substitute for 1-hr. const.; include atria; or use in an H-1, H-2, H-3, or H-7 occupancy. [506c]

4. These story limits may be increased by one story if the building is fully sprinklered, provided no other increase for sprinkling is used. [507]

5. Non-bearing walls fronting public ways or yards ≥40' wide may be non-rated, non-combust. [1803a, 1903a, 2003a, 2103a]

6. Rated shafts are not required for:

    a. Openings between one floor only, not concealed w/in building const.

    b. In type V buildings, chutes and dumbwaiters <9 sq. ft. in cross-sectional area and lined w/gyp. bd. and sheet metal.

    c. Gas vents, factory-built chimneys, and piping through two floors max.

    d. Sprinklered B occupancies need not enclose escalators that have draft curtains. [1706]

7. See Chapter 7, "Area Separations," page 80.

8. Corridors in non-rated buildings serving an occupant load <30 may be non-rated (excluding R-1 or any I occupancy). [3305g]

9. The area of any one- or two-story B or H-5 fully-sprinklered building with all yards ≥60' wide may be unlimited. [506b]

10. Roof const. (other than primary members) in type I, II-F.R., or II-1-hr. ≥25' above all floors/levels may be non-rated, non-combust. H.T. const. may be used if such building is only one story. [1806]

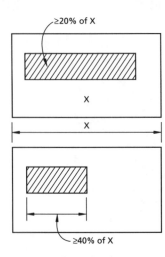

NOTE: Formulas given are per tier, not per wall.

Figure 2.2
Open Parking Garage Opening.

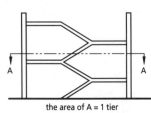

the area of A = 1 tier
(a) sloping floors

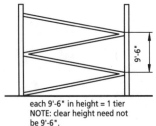

each 9'-6" in height = 1 tier
NOTE: clear height need not be 9'-6".
(b) continuous spiral floors

Figure 2.3
Open Parking Garage Tier Areas.

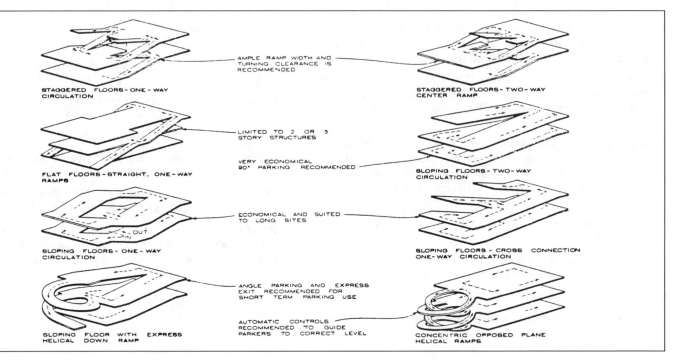

Figure 2.1
Open Parking Garage Configurations.
From *Architectural Graphic Standards*, 8th Edition; Charles G. Ramsey & Harold R. Sleeper, copyright © 1988 by John Wiley & Sons, Inc. Reprinted by permission of John Wiley & Sons, Inc.

Definition [709]

An open parking garage is: Type I or II construction

and

Used exclusively for the parking or storage of private vehicles (no parking of buses or trucks, and no repair work).

(See Figure 2.1 for typical open parking garage configurations.)

Natural Ventilation/Openings [709b]

The total **area** of openings on each tier must be ≥20 percent of the **area** of the perimeter wall on each tier.

and

The total **length** of openings on each tier must be ≥40 percent of the **length** of each tier.

(See Figure 2.2.)

Construction [709c]

Exterior walls: 1-hr. if <10' from p/l.

Openings: Not allowed <5' from p/l, 3/4 hr. if <10' from p/l.

Clear Height [709d]

7'-0" minimum clear height.

NOTE: A lesser clear height may be approved by the building official for garages with auto-lifts.

Core/Office Areas Within Structures [709b]

The grade level tier may contain office, waiting, and toilet rooms with a combined total area ≤**1,000 sq. ft.**

Positive pressurization of these rooms is required.

Area Calculations [709d]

To determine the area of a tier in parking structures with:

Sloping floors: The horizontal cross-sectional area = 1 tier.

Continuous spiral floors: Each 9'-6" in height = 1 tier.

(See Figure 2.3.)

Table 2.3 **Parking Garage Area and Height**

Type of Const.	Max Sq. Ft. Per Tier	Maximum Height		
		Ramp Access	Garages w/Auto-Lifts	
			Unsprinklered	Sprinklered
I	Unlimited	Unlimited	Unlimited	Unlimited
II F.R.	125,000	12 tiers	12 tiers	18 tiers
II-1-Hr.	50,000	10 tiers	10 tiers	15 tiers
II N	30,000	8 tiers	8 tiers	12 tiers

Exceptions to Table 2.3 [709e]

Type II structures with all sides open: May be unlimited in area if their height is ≤75'.

NOTE: For a side to be considered "open" under *this exception*, the total **area** of openings along the side must be ≥50 percent of the **exterior area of that tier**. (See Figure 2.4.) Openings must be equally distributed. All portions of tiers must be within 200' of such openings.

All structures with sides open on ³/₄ of the building perimeter: May increase their maximum allowed area by **25 percent** and maximum allowed height by **one tier**.

All structures with sides open on all of the building perimeter: May increase their maximum allowed area by **50 percent** and maximum allowed height by **one tier**.

NOTE: For a side to be considered "open" under *the previous two exceptions*, the total **area** of openings must be ≥50 percent of the **interior area along the side at each tier**. (See Figure 2.5.) Such openings must be equally distributed.

Structures lower than the max. allowed height: May have individual tier areas > those otherwise allowed, provided the **gross tier area** is ≤ the **total** area allowed for the higher garage (a garage at max. allowed height). At least **three sides** of each such larger tier must have **continuous openings ≥30" high for ≥80 percent of the length** of the side. (See Figure 2.6.)

All parts of each such tier must be within 200' of these openings. Each tier face must adjoin a minimum **30' wide yard/public way**. Standpipes must be provided at each tier.

Stairs and Exits [709g]

Stairs and exits shall be computed as for a **B-3 occupancy** with an **occupant load of 200.** (See Chapter 8.)

Where no persons other than parking attendants are allowed: There must be a minimum of two stairs ≥36" wide.

Auto-lifts may be installed for use of employees only, provided they are completely enclosed by non-combustible materials.

Sprinkler Systems [709i]

Sprinkler systems must be provided when required by any other provision of the code. (See Tables 2.2 and 2.3.)

Vertical Opening Enclosure [709j]

Vertical opening enclosure is not required, except as described for auto-lifts.

Ventilation [709k]

Other than the percentage of openings required (see "Natural Ventilation/Openings"), additional ventilation is not required.

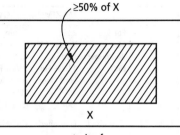

Figure 2.4
Open Parking Garage Open Side for Area and Height Exception.

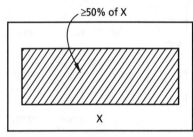

Figure 2.5
Open Parking Garage Open Side for Area and Height Exception.

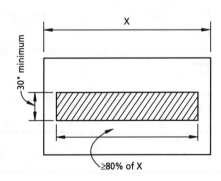

Figure 2.6
Open Parking Garage Open Side for Area and Height Exception.

Table 2.4 B-4 Commercial Occupancy

B-4	MAXIMUM ALLOWABLE SQ. FT.					Maximum Building Height[4] [5D,507]	CONSTRUCTION (FIRE-RESISTIVE REQUIREMENTS IN HOURS)											
	For 1 Story Buildings[1] [5C]	2 Side Yards >20' Add 1¼% Per Foot Over 20'[2] [506a]	3 Side Yards >20' Add 2½% Per Foot Over 20'[2] [506a]	All Side Yards >20' Add 5% Per Foot Over 20'[2] [506c]	Additional Sq. Ft. If Sprinklered[3] [506c]		Exterior Bearing Walls [17A]	Interior Bearing Walls [17A]	Exterior Non-bearing Walls	Structural Frame [17A]	Permanent Partitions [17A]	Shaft Enclosures [17A]	Floors/ Ceilings [17A]	Roofs/ Ceilings [17A]	Exterior Doors & Windows	Area Separation Walls[10] [505f]	Exit Corridors [3305g]	Exit Stairways [3306l]
Type I	Unlimited	Unlimited	Unlimited	Unlimited	Unlimited	Unlimited	2 hr., <5' fm. p/l 4 hr.	3 hr.	1 hr., <5' fm. p/l 4 hr.[5]	3 hr.	1 hr.	2 hr.	2 hr.	2 hr.[10]	<20' fm. p/l 1¾ hr., N.A. <3' fm. p/l [1803b]	4 hr.	1 hr.	2 hr.
II F.R.	59,900	89,850	119,000	119,000	1 & 2 stories × 3, >2 story × 2[9]	12 stories 160'	"	2 hr.	"	2 hr.	1 hr.	2 hr.	2 hr.	1 hr.[10]	" [1903b]	4 hr.	1 hr.	2 hr.
II 1-HR	27,000	40,500	54,000	54,000	"	4 stories 65'	1 hr. [5A]	1 hr.	1 hr.[5] [5A]	1 hr.	1 hr.	1 hr.	1 hr.	1 hr.[10]	N.A., <5' fm. p/l [5A]	2 hr.	1 hr.	1 hr., ≥ 4 stories 2 hr.
II N	18,000	27,000	36,000	36,000	"	2 stories 55'	None, <5' fm. p/l 1 hr. [5A]	None	None, <5' fm. p/l 1 hr.[5] [5A]	None	None	1 hr.	None	None	"	2 hr.	1 hr.[8]	"
III 1-HR	27,000	40,500	54,000	54,000	"	4 stories 65'	2 hr., <5' fm. p/l 4 hr.	1 hr.	1 hr., <5' fm. p/l 4 hr.[5]	1 hr.	1 hr.	1 hr.	1 hr.	1 hr.	<20' fm. p/l 1¾ hr., N.A. <3' fm. p/l [2003b]	4 hr.	1 hr.	"
III N	18,000	27,000	36,000	36,000	"	2 stories 55'	"	None	"	None	None	1 hr.	None	None	"	4 hr.	1 hr.[8]	"
IV H.T.	27,000	40,500	54,000	54,000	"	4 stories 65'	"	1 hr.	"	1 hr. or H.T.	1 hr. or H.T.	1 hr.	H.T.	H.T.	" [2103b]	4 hr.	1 hr.	"
V 1-HR	21,000	31,500	42,000	42,000	"	3 stories 50'	1 hr. [5A]	1 hr.	1 hr. [5A]	1 hr.	1 hr.	1 hr.[6]	1 hr.	1 hr.	N.A., <5' fm. p/l [5A]	2 hr.	1 hr.	"
V N	12,000	18,000	24,000	24,000	"	2 stories 40'	None, <5' fm. p/l 1 hr. [5A]	None	None, <5' fm. p/l 1 hr. [5A]	None	None	1 hr.[6]	None	None	"	2 hr.	1 hr.[8]	"

1. The total combined area for multistory buildings may be 2× that shown, and the area of any single story must be ≤ that given above. **Figures given are maximums.** [505]

2. The maximum floor areas given "FOR 1 STORY BUILDINGS" may be increased where public ways or yards are ≥20' wide, according to the **rates** given here. **Figures given are maximums.** [506a]

3. The multiplying factor given here (a doubling or tripling of allowed sq. ft.) shall not apply when sprinklers are used to: increase the number of stories; substitute for 1-hr. const.; include atria; or use in an H-1, H-2, H-3, or H-7 occupancy. [506c]

4. These story limits may be increased by one story if the building is fully sprinklered, provided no other increase for sprinkling is used. [507]

5. Non-bearing walls fronting public ways or yards ≥40' wide may be non-rated, non-combust. [1803a, 1903a, 2003a, 2103a]

6. Rated shafts are not required for:

   a. Openings between one floor only, not concealed w/in building const.

   b. In type V buildings, chutes and dumbwaiters <9 sq. ft. in cross-sectional area and lined w/gyp. bd. and sheet metal.

   c. Gas vents, factory-built chimneys, and piping through two floors max.

   d. Sprinklered B occupancies need not enclose escalators that have draft curtains. [1706]

7. See Chapter 7, "Area Separations," page 80.

8. Corridors in non-rated buildings serving an occupant load <30 may be non-rated (excluding R-1 or any I occupancy). [3305g]

9. The area of any one- or two-story B or H-5 fully-sprinklered building with all yards ≥60' wide may be unlimited. [506b]

10. Roof const. (other than primary members) in type I, II-F.R., or II-1-hr. ≥25' above all floors/levels may be non-rated, non-combust. H.T. const. may be used if such building is only one story. [1806]

General Sanitation [510]

Water closet rooms: Must be separated from food preparation/storage areas by a tight-fitting door.

Floors and walls in water closet rooms and showers: Must be of smooth, non-absorbant, hard finishes.

Walls must be so finished up to a minimum 48".

Shower walls must be so finished up to a minimum 70".

Floor base must be a minimum 5".

Light [705]

All occupied rooms must have either: Window opening(s) $\geq 1/10$ the floor area of the room.

or

Artificial light.

Ventilation [705]

All occupied rooms must have either: Openable window(s) with an area $\geq 1/20$ the floor area of the room.

or

Mechanical ventilation.

Toilet Rooms [705]

Toilet rooms must have ventilation by either: Openable window(s) ≥ 3 sq. ft.

or

Mechanical ventilation.

At least one lavatory and one water closet must be provided.

Separate facilities for each sex must be provided when the number of employees >4.

Barrier-free access: ≥ 1 of each sanitary fixture provided per floor must be accessible.

UPC recommended:

Office-Employee Use (fixtures:persons)

Water Closets	Urinals	Lavs
1:1–15	1:50	1:40
2:16–35		
3:36–55		
>55 persons, add 1:40 persons		

Office-Public Use

Water Closets	Lavs
1:1–15	1:1–15
2:16–35	2:16–35
3:36–55	3:36–60
4:56–80	4:61–90
5:81–110	5:91–125
6:111–150	>125 persons, add 1:45
>150 persons, add 1:40 persons	

UPC recommended:

Restaurants/Bars

Water Closets Male	Female	Urinals	Lavs
1:1–50	1:1–50	1:1–150	1:1–150
2:51–150	2:51–150	>150, add	2:151–200
3:151–300	4:151–300	1:150	3:201–400
>300, add 1:200 addit. persons		addit. males	>400, add 1:400 addit. persons

Industrial/Warehouse

Water Closets

1:1–10

2:11–25

3:26–50

4:51–75

5:76–100

>100 persons, add 1:30 addit. persons

Lavs

1:10 persons up to 100 persons,

1:15 over 100 persons

Drinking Fountains

Not required.

Barrier-free access: If provided, ≥1 fountain per floor must be accessible to those in wheelchairs, and ≥1 fountain must be accessible to those who have difficulty bending.

UPC recommended: 1:75 persons.

3

E Occupancies

Table 3.1 E (All) Educational Occupancies

B-1 & B-2	MAXIMUM ALLOWABLE SQ. FT.					Maximum Building Height [4] [5D,507]	CONSTRUCTION (FIRE-RESISTIVE REQUIREMENTS IN HOURS)											
	For 1 Story Buildings[1] [5C]	2 Side Yards >20' Add 1¼% Per Foot Over 20'[2] [506a]	3 Side Yards >20' Add 2½% Per Foot Over 20'[2] [506a]	All Side Yards >20' Add 5% Per Foot Over 20'[2] [506a]	Additional Sq. Ft. If Sprinklered[3] [506c]		Exterior Bearing Walls [17A]	Interior Bearing Walls [17A]	Exterior Non-bearing Walls	Structural Frame [17A]	Permanent Partitions [17A]	Shaft Enclosures [17A]	Floors/Ceilings [17A]	Roofs/Ceilings [17A]	Exterior Doors & Windows	Area Separation Walls [10] [505f]	Exit Corridors [3305g]	Exit Stairways [3306l]
Type I	Unlimited	Unlimited	Unlimited	Unlimited	Unlimited	Unlimited	4 hr.	3 hr.	1 hr., <10' fm. p/l 2 hr., <5' fm. p/l 4 hr.[5]	3 hr.	1 hr.	2 hr.	2 hr.	2 hr.[7]	<20' fm. p/l 1¾ hr., N.A. <5' fm. p/l [1803b]	4 hr.	1 hr.	2 hr.
II F.R.	45,200[12]	67,800	90,400	90,400	1 story × 3, >1 story × 2	4 stories 160'	4 hr.	2 hr.	"	2 hr.	1 hr.	2 hr.	2 hr.	1 hr.[7]	" [1903b]	4 hr.	1 hr.	2 hr.
II 1-HR	20,200[12]	30,300	40,400	40,400	"	2 stories 65'	1 hr., <5' fm. p/l 2 hr. [5A]	1 hr.	1 hr., <5' fm. p/l 2 hr.[5]	1 hr.	1 hr.	1 hr.	1 hr.	1 hr.[7]	<10' fm. p/l 1¾ hr., N.A. <5' fm. p/l [5A]	2 hr.	1 hr.	1 hr., ≥ 4 stories 2 hr.
II N	13,500[12]	20,250	27,000	27,000	"	1 story 55'	None, <10' fm. p/l 1 hr., <5' fm. p/l 2 hr. [5A]	None	None, <10' fm. p/l 1 hr., <5' fm. p/l 2 hr.[5] [5A]	None	None	1 hr.	None	None	" [5A]	2 hr.	1 hr.[9]	"
III 1-HR	20,200[12]	30,300	40,400	40,400	"	2 stories 65'	4 hr.	1 hr.	1 hr., <10' fm. p/l 2 hr., <5' fm. p/l 4 hr.[5]	1 hr.	1 hr.	1 hr.	1 hr.	1 hr.	<20' fm. p/l 1¾ hr., N.A. <5' fm. p/l [2003b]	4 hr.	1 hr.	"
III N	13,500[12]	20,250	27,000	27,000	"	1 story 55'	4 hr.	None	"	None	None	1 hr.	None	None	" [2003b]	4 hr.	1 hr.[9]	"
IV H.T.	20,200[12]	30,300	40,400	40,400	"	2 stories 65'	4 hr.	1 hr.	"	1 hr. or H.T.	1 hr. or H.T.	1 hr.	H.T.	H.T.	" [2103b]	4 hr.	1 hr.	"
V 1-HR	15,700[12]	23,550	31,400	31,400	"	2 stories 50'	1 hr., <5' fm. p/l 2 hr. [5A]	1 hr.	1 hr., <5' fm. p/l 2 hr.[5] [5A]	1 hr.	1 hr.	1 hr.[6]	1 hr.	1 hr.	<10' fm. p/l 1¾ hr., N.A. <5' fm. p/l [5A]	2 hr.	1 hr.	"
V N	9,100[12]	13,650	18,200	18,200	"	1 story 40'	None, <10' fm. p/l 1 hr., <5' fm. p/l 2 hr. [5A]	None	None, <10' fm. p/l 1 hr., <5' fm. p/l 2 hr.[5] [5A]	None	None	1 hr.[6]	None	None	" [5A]	2 hr.	1 hr.[9]	"

1. The total combined area for multistory buildings may be 2× that shown, and the area of any single story must be ≤ that given above. **Figures given are maximums.** [505]

2. The maximum floor areas given "FOR 1 STORY BUILDINGS" may be increased where public ways or yards are ≥20' wide, according to the **rates** given here. **Figures given are maximums.** [506a]

3. The multiplying factor given here (a doubling or tripling of allowed sq. ft.) shall not apply when sprinklers are used to: increase the number of stories; substitute for 1-hr. const.; include atria; or use in an H-1, H-2, H-3, or H-7 occupancy. [506c]

4. These story limits may be increased by one story if the building is fully sprinklered, provided no other increase for sprinkling is used. [507]

5. Non-bearing walls fronting public ways or yards ≥40' wide may be non-rated, non-combust. [1803a, 1903a, 2003a, 2103a]

6. Rated shafts are not required for:

   a. Openings between one floor only, not concealed w/in building const.

   b. In type V buildings, chutes and dumbwaiters <9 sq. ft. in cross-sectional area and lined w/gyp. bd. and sheet metal.

   c. Gas vents, factory-built chimneys, and piping through two floors max. [1706]

7. a. Roof const., including primary struct., ≥25' above all floors/levels in type I, II-F.R., II-1-hr., or an atrium may be non-rated.

   b. Ceilings in A or E occupancies of type I, II-F.R., or II-1-hr. >18' but <25' above all floors/levels may be only 1-hr. [1806]

8. See Chapter 7, "Area Separations," page 80.

9. Corridors in non-rated buildings serving <30 occupants may be non-rated. [3305g]

10. E-2 and E-3 buildings w/≤20 occupants may have unprotected openings ≥3' from p/l. [5A]

11. Every room in E occupancies w/≥300 occupants must have one of its exits into a separate exit system (one w/complete atmospheric separation). [3318b]

12. Area may be increased by 50 percent if max. distance to exits is decreased by 50 percent. [802]

General Sanitation [510]

Water closet rooms: Must be separated from food preparation/storage areas by a tight-fitting door.

Floors and walls in water closet rooms and showers: Must be of smooth, non-absorbant, hard finishes.

Walls must be so finished up to a minimum 48".

Shower walls must be so finished up to a minimum 70".

Floor base must be a minimum 5".

Light [805]

All occupied rooms must have either: Window opening(s) $\geq 1/10$ the floor area of the room.

or

Artificial light.

Ventilation [805]

All occupied rooms must have either: Openable window(s) with an area $\geq 1/20$ the floor area of the room.

or

Mechanical ventilation.

Toilet Rooms [805]

Toilet rooms must have ventilation by either: Openable window(s) ≥ 3 sq. ft.

or

Mechanical ventilation.

At least one lavatory for every two water closets for each sex must be provided.

Minimum fixture requirements:

| Water Closets | | Urinals |
Male	Female	
1:100	1:35	1:30

Barrier free access: ≥ 1 of each sanitary fixture provided per floor must be accessible.

UPC recommended: (fixtures:persons)

Staff Use

Water Closets	Urinals	Lavs
1:1–15	1:50	1:40
2:16–35		
3:36–55		
>55 persons, add 1:40 persons		

UPC recommended: (fixtures:persons)

Student Use
Nursery

Water Closets	Lavs
1:1–20	1:1–25
2:21–50	2:26–50
over 50 persons, add 1:50 addit. persons	

Elementary

| Water Closets | | Urinals | Lavs |
Male	Female		
1:30	1:25	1:75	1:35

Secondary/Higher

| Water Closets | | Urinals | Lavs |
Male	Female		
1:40	1:30	1:35	1:40

Drinking Fountains [805]

At least one drinking fountain per floor must be provided.

Barrier free access: ≥ 1 fountain per floor must be accessible to those in wheelchairs, and ≥ 1 fountain must be accessible to those who have difficulty bending.

UPC recommended: 1:75 persons.

4

H Occupancies

H Occupancy Definitions [901]

H occupancies are defined by the **kind and quantity** of hazardous material being used/stored.

It is necessary to know the exact nature and quantity of materials that will be used/stored in the building prior to defining its occupancy.

H-1 (High explosive hazard)

Buildings that house:

a. Explosives, blasting agents, fireworks, or black powder.

Exception: 90-day max. storage of pyrotechnic materials used in entertainment production—with special permit as required by the fire code.

b. Unclassified detonatable organic peroxides.

c. Class 4 oxidizers.

d. Class 4 or Class 3 detonatable unstable (reactive) materials.

(See Tables 4.1 and 4.2 for exempt amounts of hazardous materials.)

(See Table 4.3 for min. distance from p/l for buildings w/ explosives.)

Special requirements: H-1 occupancies must be in buildings used for no other purpose.

H-1 buildings may have no basements, crawl spaces, or any under-floor spaces.

H-2 (Explosion/accelerated burning hazard)

Buildings that house:

a. Class I organic peroxides.

b. Class 3 non-detonatable unstable (reactive) materials.

c. Pyrophoric gases.

d. Flammable or oxidizing gases.

e. Class I, II, or II-A flammable or combustible liquids used/stored in open containers or in closed containers pressurized at >15 lbs. per sq. in. gauge.

Exception: Aerosols.

f. Combustible dust in suspension or capable of being put into suspension in the room or area.

Exceptions: Woodworking rooms with ≤3 woodworking appliances w/combined exhaust requirements <1,000 cu. ft. per minute may be classified as B-2 occupancies, provided the woodworking appliances are equipped with dust collectors capable of removing all of the dust generated by the appliances.

Lumberyards and similar retail buildings using only power saws may be classified as B-2 occupancies.

g. Class 3 oxidizers.

(See Tables 4.1 and 4.2 for exempt amounts of hazardous materials.)

(See Table 4.3 for min. distance from p/l for buildings w/ explosives.)

Special requirements: H-2 occupancies must be in buildings used for no other purpose.

H-2 buildings may have no basements, crawl spaces, or any under-floor spaces.

H-3 (High fire or physical hazard)

Buildings that house:

a. Class II, III, or IV organic peroxides.

b. Class 1 or 2 oxidizers.

c. Class I, II, or III-A flammable or combustible liquids used/stored in closed containers or containers pressurized at ≤15 lbs. per sq. in. gauge or aerosols.

d. Class III-B combustible liquids.

e. Pyrophoric liquids or solids.

f. Water reactives.

g. Flammable solids, including combustible fibers or dusts, except for dusts described in H-2 occupancies.

h. Flammable or oxidizing cryogenic fluids (not inert).

i. Class 1 unstable (reactive) gas or Class 2 unstable (reactive) matter.

(See Tables 4.1 and 4.2 for exempt amounts of hazardous materials.)

Special requirements: H-3 occupancies must be in buildings used for no other purpose.

H-3 buildings may have no basements, crawl spaces, or any under-floor spaces.

H-4

Repair garages not allowed in B-1 occupancies.

H-5

Aircraft repair hangars and heliports not allowed in B-3 occupancies.

H-6 (Semiconductor fabrication facilities)

Buildings that house:

Semiconductor fabrication facilities and similar research/development facilities where hazardous production materials are used.

(See Tables 4.1 and 4.2 for exempt amounts of hazardous materials.)

Special requirements:

Area: Fabrication area maximum allowable sq. ft. is limited by the local fire code.

Separation: Fabrication areas within the same building must be **separated from:**

each other

and

exit corridors

and

other parts of the building

by a ≥1-hr. occupancy separation.

Service corridors: Hazardous production materials must be transported in separate service corridors, *not in exit corridors*.

Service corridors must be separated from exit corridors by a ≥1-hr. occupancy separation.

Maximum distance to exits in a service corridor must be ≤75'.

Dead-ends in service corridors must be ≤4'.

There must be ≥2 exits from a service corridor.

Storage rooms for hazardous production material: Storage of hazardous production material in amounts >Table ref. 3.1 must be in rooms of H-6 occupancy ≤**6,000 sq. ft.**

Such storage rooms must be of **2-hr.** const. when ≥300 sq. ft., and **1-hr.** const. if <300 sq. ft.

If such storage rooms are also used to store Class I or II flammable liquids or gases, they must be ≤1,000 sq. ft.

Such storage rooms must have at least **one exterior wall and be ≥30' from any p/l.**

If ≥2 exits are required from such storage rooms, ≥1 must lead directly outside.

H-7 (Health hazards)

Buildings that house:

a. Corrosives

b. Toxics

c. Sensitizers

d. Other health hazards

(See Table 4.2 for exempt amounts of hazardous materials.)

Class I, II, and III-A flammable or combustible liquid use/dispensing/mixing rooms

Such **rooms** are classified as **H-2** and must meet the following **additional requirements**:

1. Rooms >**500 sq. ft.** must have at least one exterior door approved for fire dept. access.

and

2. Rooms must be ≤1,000 sq. ft.

and

3. Rooms ≤**150 sq. ft.** must be separated from other areas by a **1-hr.** occupancy separation.

and

4. Rooms >**150 sq. ft.** must be separated from other areas by a **2-hr.** occupancy separation.

and

5. Such rooms must not be located in basements.

Class I, II, and III-A flammable or combustible liquid storage rooms

Such **rooms** are classified as **H-3** occupancy and must meet the following **additional requirements**:

1. Rooms >**500 sq. ft.** must have at least one exterior door approved for fire dept. access.

and

2. Rooms must be ≤1,000 sq. ft.

and

3. Rooms ≤ **150 sq. ft.** must be separated from other areas by a **1-hr.** occupancy separation.

and

4. Rooms >150 sq. ft. must be separated from other areas by a 2-hr. occupancy separation.

and

5. Such rooms must not be located in basements.

Class I, II, and III-A liquid storage warehouses

Such **warehouses** are classified as **H-3** occupancies and must meet the following **additional requirements**:

1. Such warehouses must be separated from all other uses by a **4-hr.** area separation wall.

and

2. Such warehouses must not be located in basements.

Table 4.1 Exempt Amounts of Hazardous Materials, Liquids, and Chemicals Presenting a Physical Hazard Basic Quantities Per Control Area[1] [9A]

When two units are given, values within parentheses are in cubic feet (cu. ft.) or pounds (lbs.)

Condition / Materials	Class	Storage[2] Solid Lbs.[3] (Cu. Ft.)	Liquid Gallons[3] (Lbs.)	Gas Cu. Ft.	Use[2]—Closed Systems Solid Lbs. (Cu. Ft.)	Liquid Gallons (Lbs.)	Gas Cu. Ft.	Use[2]—Open Systems Solid Lbs. (Cu. Ft)	Liquid Gallons (Lbs.)
1.1 Combustible liquid [4,5,6,8,9,10]	II	N.A.	120[7]	N.A.	N.A.	120	N.A.	N.A.	30
	III-A	N.A.	330[7]	N.A.	N.A.	330	N.A.	N.A.	80
	III-B	N.A.	13,200[7,11]	N.A.	N.A.	13,200[11]	N.A.	N.A.	3,300[11]
1.2 Combustible dust lbs./1000 cu. ft.[12]		1	N.A.	N.A.	1	N.A.	N.A.	1	N.A.
1.3 Combustible fiber (loose)		(100)	N.A.	N.A.	(100)	N.A.	N.A.	(20)	N.A.
(baled)		(1,000)	N.A.	N.A.	(1,000)	N.A.	N.A.	(200)	N.A.
1.4 Cryogenic, flammable or oxidizing			45	N.A.	N.A.	45	N.A.	N.A.	10
2.1 Explosives[13]		1[7,14]	(1)[7,14]	N.A.	1/4	(1/4)	N.A.	1/4	(1/4)
3.1 Flammable solid		125[6,7]	N.A.	N.A.	25[6]	N.A.	N.A.	25[6]	N.A.
3.2 Flammable gas (gaseous)		N.A.	N.A.	750[6,7]	N.A.	N.A.	750[6,7]	N.A.	N.A.
(liquefied)		N.A.	15[7]	N.A.	N.A.	15[6,7]	N.A.	N.A.	N.A.
3.3 Flammable liquid [4,5,6,9,10]	I-A	N.A.	30[7]	N.A.	N.A.	30	N.A.	N.A.	10
	I-B	N.A.	60[7]	N.A.	N.A.	60	N.A.	N.A.	15
	I-C	N.A.	90[7]	N.A.	N.A.	90	N.A.	N.A.	20
Combination I-A, I-B, I-C		N.A.	120[7]	N.A.	N.A.	120	N.A.	N.A.	30
4.1 Organic peroxide, unclassified detonatable		1[7,13]	(1)[7,13]	N.A.	1/4[13]	(1/4)[13]	N.A.	1/4[13]	(1/4)[13]
4.2 Organic peroxide	I	5[6,7]	(5)[6,7]	N.A.	(1)[6]	(1)[6]	N.A.	1[6]	1[6]
	II	50[6,7]	(50)[6,7]	N.A.	50[6]	(50)[6]	N.A.	10[6]	(10)[6]
	III	125[6,7]	(125)[6,7]	N.A.	125[6]	(125)[6]	N.A.	25[6]	(25)[6]
	IV	500	(500)	N.A.	500[6]	(500)	N.A.	100	(100)
	V	N.L.	N.L.	N.A.	N.L.	N.L.	N.A.	N.L.	N.L.
4.3 Oxidizer	4	1[7,13]	(1)[7,13]	N.A.	1/4[13]	(1/4)[13]	N.A.	1/4[13]	(1/4)[13]
	3[16]	10[6,7]	(10)[6,7]	N.A.	2[6]	(2)[6]	N.A.	2[6]	(2)[6]
	2	250[6,7]	(250)[6,7]	N.A.	250[6]	(250)[6]	N.A.	50[6]	(50)[6]
	1	4,000[6,7]	(4,000)[6,7]	N.A.	4,000[6]	(4,000)[6]	N.A.	1,000[6]	(1,000)[6]
4.4 Oxidizer—Gas (gaseous)[6,7]		N.A.	N.A.	1,500	N.A.	N.A.	1,500	N.A.	N.A.
(liquefied)[6,7]		N.A.	15	N.A.	N.A.	15	N.A.	N.A.	N.A.
5.1 Pyrophoric		4[7,13]	(4)[7,13]	50[7,13]	1[13]	(1)[13]	10[7,13]	0	0
6.1 Unstable (reactive)	4	1[7,13]	(1)[7,13]	10[7,13]	1/4[13]	(1/4)[13]	2[7,13]	1/4[13]	(1/4)[13]
	3	5[6,7]	(5)[6,7]	50[6,7]	1[6]	(1)[6]	10[4,5]	1[6]	(1)[6]
	2	50[6,7]	(50)[6,7]	250[6,7]	50[6]	(50)[6]	250[4,5]	10[6]	(10)[6]
	1	N.L.	N.L.	750[6,7]	N.L.	N.L.	N.L.	N.L.	(25)[6]
7.1 Water (reactive)	3	5[6,7]	(5)[6,7]	N.A.	5[6]	(5)[6]	N.A.	1[6]	(1)[6]
	2	50[6,7]	(50)[6,7]	N.A.	50[6]	(50)[6]	N.A.	10[6]	(10)[6]
	1	125[7,11]	(125)[7,11]	N.A.	125[11]	(125)[7,11]	N.A.	25[11]	(25)[11]

N.A.= Not Applicable.   N.L.= Not Limited.

1. Control area is a space bounded by not less than a one-hour fire-resistive occupancy separation within which the exempted amounts of hazardous materials may be stored, dispensed, handled, or used. The number of control areas within a building used for retail and wholesale stores shall not exceed two. The number of control areas in buildings with other uses shall not exceed four.

2. The aggregate quantity in use and storage shall not exceed the quantity listed for storage.

3. The aggregate quantity of nonflammable solid and nonflammable or noncombustible liquid hazardous materials within a single control area of Group B. Division 2 Occupancies used for retail sales may exceed the exempt amounts when such areas are in compliance with the Fire Code.

4. The quantities of alcoholic beverages in retail sales uses are unlimited provided the liquids are packaged in individual containers not exceeding four liters.

    The quantities of medicines, foodstuffs, and cosmetics containing not more than 50 percent of volume of water-miscible liquids and with the remainder of the solutions not being flammable in retail sales or storage occupancies are unlimited when packaged in individual containers not exceeding four liters.

5. For aerosols, see the Fire Code.

6. Quantities may be increased 100 percent in sprinklered buildings. When Footnote No. 7 also applies, the increase for both footnotes may be applied.

7. Quantities may be increased 100 percent when stored in approved storage cabinets, gas cabinets, fume hoods, exhaust enclosures, or safety cans as specified in the Fire Code. When Footnote No. 6 also applies, the increase for both footnotes may be applied.

8. For wholesale and retail sales use, also see the Fire Code.

9. Spray application of any quantity of flammable or combustible liquids shall be conducted as set forth in the Fire Code.

10. The quantities permitted in a sprinklered building are not limited.

11. A dust explosion potential is considered to exist if 1 pound or more of combustible dust per 1,000 cubic feet of volume is normally in suspension or could be put into suspension in all or a portion of an enclosure or inside pieces of equipment. This also includes combustible dust which accumulates on horizontal surfaces inside buildings or equipment and which could be put into suspension by an accident, sudden force, or small explosion.

12. Permitted in sprinklered buildings only. None is allowed in unsprinklered buildings.

13. One pound of black sporting powder and 20 pounds of smokeless powder are permitted in sprinklered or unsprinklered buildings.

14. Containing not more than the exempt amounts of Class I-A, Class I-B, or Class I-C flammable liquids.

15. A maximum quantity of 200 pounds of solid or 20 gallons of liquid Class 3 oxidizers may be permitted in Groups I, M, and R Occupancies when such materials are necessary for maintenance purposes or operation of equipment as set forth in the Fire Code.

Table 4.2 **Exempt Amounts of Hazardous Materials, Liquids, and Chemicals Presenting A Health Hazard. Maximum Quantities Per Control Area[1,2] [9B]**

When two units are given, values within parentheses are in pounds (lbs.)

Material	Storage[3]			Use[3]—Closed Systems			Use[3]—Open Systems	
	Solid Lbs.[4,5,6]	Liquid Gallons[4,5,6] (Lbs.)	Gas Cu. Ft.[5]	Solid Lbs.[4,5]	Liquid Gallons[4,5] (Lbs.)	Gas Cu. Ft.	Solid Lbs.[4,5]	Liquid Gallons[4,5] (Lbs.)
1. Corrosives	5,000	500	650[6]	5,000	500	650[5,6]	1,000	100
2. Highly toxics[8]	1	(1)	20[7]	1	(1)	20[7]	1/4	(1/4)
3. Irritants	5,000	500	650[6]	5,000	500	650[5,6]	1,000	100
4. Sensitizers	5,000	500	650[6]	5,000	500	650[5,6]	1,000	100
5. Other health hazards	5,000	500	650[6]	5,000	500	650[5,6]	1,000	100
6. Toxics	500	(500)	650[6]	500	(500)	20[5,7]	125	(125)

1. Control area is a space bounded by not less than one-hour fire-resistive occupancy separation within which the exempted amounts of hazardous materials may be stored, dispensed, handled, or used. The number of control areas within retail and wholesale stores shall not exceed two and the number of control areas in other uses shall not exceed four.

2. The quantities of medicines, foodstuffs, and cosmetics, containing not more than 50 percent by volume of water-miscible liquids and with the remainder of the solutions not being flammable, in retail sales uses are unlimited when packaged in individual containers not exceeding 4 liters.

3. The aggregate quantity in use and storage shall not exceed the quantity listed for storage.

4. The aggregate quantity of nonflammable solid and nonflammable or noncombustible liquid health hazard materials within a single control area of Group B, Division 2 Occupancies used for retail sales may exceed the exempt amounts when such areas are in compliance with the Fire Code.

5. Quantities may be increased 100 percent in sprinklered buildings. When Footnote No. 6 also applies, the increase for both footnotes may be applied.

6. Quantities may be increased 100 percent when stored in approved storage cabinets, gas cabinets, fume hoods, exhausted enclosures, or safety cans as specified in the Fire Code. When Footnote No. 5 also applies, the increase for both footnotes may be applied.

7. Permitted only when stored in approved exhausted gas cabinets, exhausted enclosures, or fume hoods.

8. For special provisions, see the Fire Code.

Table 4.3 **Minimum Distances for Buildings Containing Explosive Materials. [9D]**

Quantity of Explosive Material[1] (Lbs)		Minimum Distance (Feet)			Quantity of Explosive Material[1] (Lbs)		Minimum Distance (Feet)			Quantity of Explosive Material[1] (Lbs)		Minimum Distance (Feet)		
Over	Not Over	Property Lines[2] and Inhabited Buildings[3]		Separation of Magazines [4,5,6]	Over	Not Over	Property Lines[2] and Inhabited Buildings[3]		Separation of Magazines [4,5,6]	Over	Not Over	Property Lines[2] and Inhabited Buildings[3]		Separation of Magazines [4,5,6]
		Barricaded[4]	Unbarricaded				Barricaded[4]	Unbarricaded				Barricaded[4]	Unbarricaded	
2	5	70	140	12	1,800	2,000	505	1,010	90	60,000	65,000	1,565	2,000	300
5	10	90	180	16	2,000	2,500	545	1,090	98	65,000	70,000	1,610	2,000	310
10	20	110	220	20	2,500	3,000	580	1,160	104	70,000	75,000	1,655	2,000	320
20	30	125	250	22	3,000	4,000	635	1,270	116	75,000	80,000	1,695	2,000	330
30	40	140	280	24	4,000	5,000	685	1,370	122	80,000	85,000	1,730	2,000	340
40	50	150	300	28	5,000	6,000	730	1,460	130	85,000	90,000	1,760	2,000	350
50	75	170	340	30	6,000	7,000	770	1,540	136	90,000	95,000	1,790	2,000	360
75	100	190	380	32	7,000	8,000	800	1,600	144	95,000	100,000	1,815	2,000	370
100	125	200	400	36	8,000	9,000	835	1,670	150	100,000	110,000	1,835	2,000	390
125	150	215	430	38	9,000	10,000	865	1,730	156	110,000	120,000	1,855	2,000	410
150	200	235	470	42	10,000	12,000	875	1,750	164	120,000	130,000	1,875	2,000	430
200	250	255	510	46	12,000	14,000	885	1,770	174	130,000	140,000	1,890	2,000	450
250	300	270	540	48	14,000	16,000	900	1,800	180	140,000	150,000	1,900	2,000	470
300	400	295	590	54	16,000	18,000	940	1,880	188	150,000	160,000	1,935	2,000	490
400	500	320	640	58	18,000	20,000	975	1,950	196	160,000	170,000	1,965	2,000	510
500	600	340	680	62	20,000	25,000	1,055	2,000	210	170,000	180,000	1,990	2,000	530
600	700	355	710	64	25,000	30,000	1,130	2,000	224	180,000	190,000	2,010	2,010	550
700	800	375	750	66	30,000	35,000	1,205	2,000	238	190,000	200,000	2,030	2,030	570
800	900	390	780	70	35,000	40,000	1,275	2,000	248	200,000	210,000	2,055	2,055	590
900	1,000	400	800	72	40,000	45,000	1,340	2,000	258	210,000	230,000	2,100	2,100	630
1,000	1,200	425	850	78	45,000	50,000	1,400	2,000	270	230,000	250,000	2,155	2,155	670
1,200	1,400	450	900	82	50,000	55,000	1,460	2,000	280	250,000	275,000	2,215	2,215	720
1,400	1,600	470	940	86	55,000	60,000	1,515	2,000	290	275,000	300,000	2,275	2,275	770
1,600	1,800	490	980	88										

1. The number of pounds of explosives listed is the number of pounds of trinitrotoluene (TNT) or the equivalent pounds of other explosive.

2. The distance listed is the distance to property line, including property lines at public ways.

3. Inhabited building is any building on the same property which is regularly occupied by human beings. When two or more buildings containing explosives or magazines are located on the same property, each building or magazine shall comply with the minimum distances specified from inhabited buildings, and, in addition, they should be separated from each other by not less than the distances shown for "Separation of Magazines," except that the quantity of explosive materials contained in detonator buildings or magazines shall govern in regard to the spacing of said detonator buildings or magazines from buildings or magazines containing other explosive materials. If any two or more buildings or magazines are separated from each other by less than the specified "Separation of Magazines" distances, then such two or more buildings or magazines, as a group, shall be considered as one building or magazine, and the total quantity of explosive materials stored in such group shall be treated as if the explosive were in a single building or magazine located on the site of any building or magazine of the group, and shall comply with the minimum distance specified from other magazines or inhibited buildings.

4. Barriers shall effectively screen the building containing explosives from other buildings, public ways or magazines. When mounds or riveted walls of earth are used for barriers, they shall not be less than 3 feet in thickness. A straight line from the top of any side wall of the building containing explosive materials to the eave line of any other building, magazine or a point 12 feet above the center line of a public way shall pass through the barrier.

5. A magazine is a building or structure approved for storage of explosive materials. In addition to the requirements of this code, magazines shall comply with the Fire Code.

6. The distance listed may be reduced by 50 percent when approved natural or artificial barriers are provided in accordance with the requirements in Footnote No. 4.

Table 4.4 **H-1 Hazardous Occupancy**

H-1	MAXIMUM ALLOWABLE SQ. FT.					Maximum Building Height [5D,507]	CONSTRUCTION (FIRE-RESISTIVE REQUIREMENTS IN HOURS)											
	For 1 Story Buildings[1] [5C]	2 Side Yards >20' Add 1¼% Per Foot Over 20'[2] [506a]	3 Side Yards >20' Add 2½% Per Foot Over 20'[2] [506a]	All Side Yards >20' Add 5% Per Foot Over 20'[2] [506a]	Additional Sq. Ft. If Sprinklered [506c]		Exterior Bearing Walls [9C]	Interior Bearing Walls [17A]	Exterior Non-bearing Walls [17A]	Structural Frame [17A]	Permanent Partitions [17A]	Shaft Enclosures [17A]	Floors/ Ceilings [17A]	Roofs/ Ceilings [17A]	Exterior Doors & Windows [9C]	Area Separation Walls[3] [505f]	Exit Corridors [3305g]	Exit Stairways [3306l]
Type I	15,00	22,500	30,000	30,000	None	1 story unlimited feet	4 hr.	3 hr.	None	3 hr.	1 hr.	2 hr.	2 hr.	2 hr.	None	4 hr.	1 hr.	2 hr.
II F.R.	12,400	18,600	24,800	24,800	"	1 story 160'	4 hr.	2 hr.	"	2 hr.	1 hr.	2 hr.	2 hr.	1 hr.	"	4 hr.	1 hr.	2 hr.
II 1-HR	5,600	8,400	11,200	11,200	"	1 story 65'	1 hr.	1 hr.	"	1 hr.	1 hr.	1 hr.	1 hr.	1 hr.	"	2 hr.	1 hr.	1 hr.
II N	3,700	5,500	7,400	7,400	"	1 story 55'	None	None	"	None	None	1 hr.	None	None	"	2 hr.	1 hr.[4]	None, ≥30 occupants 1 hr.

NOTES: See Tables 4.1 and 4.2 for exempt amounts of hazardous materials. For minimum distance from p/l, see Table 4.3.

1. The total combined area for multistory buildings may be 2× that shown, and the area of any single story must be ≤ that given above. **Figures given are maximums.** [505]

2. The maximum floor areas given "FOR 1 STORY BUILDINGS" may be increased where public ways or yards are ≥20' wide, according to the **rates** given here. **Figures given are maximums.** [506a]

3. See Chapter 7, "Area Separations," page 80.

4. Corridors in non-rated buildings serving an occupant load <30 may be non-rated (excluding R-1 or any I occupancy). [3305g]

Table 4.5 H-2 Hazardous Occupancy

H-2	MAXIMUM ALLOWABLE SQ. FT.					Maximum Building Height [5D,507]	CONSTRUCTION (FIRE-RESISTIVE REQUIREMENTS IN HOURS)											
	For 1 Story Buildings[1] [5C]	2 Side Yards >20' Add 1¼% Per Foot Over 20'[2] [506a]	3 Side Yards >20' Add 2½% Per Foot Over 20'[2] [506a]	All Side Yards >20' Add 5% Per Foot Over 20'[2] [506a]	Additional Sq. Ft. If Sprinklered [506c]		Exterior Bearing Walls [9C]	Interior Bearing Walls [9C]	Exterior Non-bearing Walls	Structural Frame [17A]	Permanent Partitions [17A]	Shaft Enclosures [17A]	Floors/ Ceilings [17A]	Roofs/ Ceilings [17A]	Exterior Doors & Windows [9C]	Area Separation Walls[4] [505f]	Exit Corridors [3305g]	Exit Stairways [3306l]
Type I	15,000	22,500	30,000	30,000	None	Unlimited[6]	4 hr.	3 hr.	<40' fm. p/l 1 hr., <10' fm. p/l 2 hr., <5' fm. p/l 4 hr.	3 hr.	1 hr.	2 hr.	2 hr.	2 hr.	<20' fm. p/l ¾ hr., N.A. <5' fm. p/l	4 hr.	1 hr.	2 hr.
II F.R.	12,400	18,600	24,800	24,800	"	2 stories 160'[6]	4 hr.	2 hr.	"	2 hr.	1 hr.	2 hr.	2 hr.	1 hr.	"	4 hr.	1 hr.	2 hr.
II 1-HR	5,600	8,400	11,200	11,200	"	1 story 65'	1 hr., <10' fm. p/l 2 hr., <5' fm. p/l 4 hr.	1 hr.	1 hr., <10' fm. p/l 2 hr., <5' fm. p/l 4 hr.	1 hr.	1 hr.	1 hr.	1 hr.	1 hr.	"	2 hr.	1 hr.	1 hr.
II N	3,700	5,500	7,400	7,400	"	1 story 55'	<20' fm. p/l 1 hr., <10' fm. p/l 2 hr., <5' fm. p/l 4 hr.	None	<20' fm. p/l 1 hr., <10' fm. p/l 2 hr., <5' fm. p/l 4 hr.	None	None	1 hr.	None	None	"	2 hr.	1 hr.[5]	None, ≥30 occupants 1 hr.
III 1-HR	5,600	8,400	11,200	11,200	"	1 story 65'	4 hr.	1 hr.	1 hr., <10' fm. p/l 2 hr., <5' fm. p/l 4 hr.	1 hr.	1 hr.	1 hr.	1 hr.	1 hr.	"	4 hr.	1 hr.	1 hr.
III N	3,700	5,500	7,400	7,400	"	1 story 55'	4 hr.	None	<40' fm. p/l 1 hr., <10' fm. p/l 2 hr., <5' fm. p/l 4 hr.	None	None	1 hr.	None	None	"	4 hr.	1 hr.[5]	None, ≥30 occupants 1 hr.
IV H.T.	5,600	8,400	11,200	11,200	"	1 story 65'	4 hr.	1 hr.	"	1 hr. or H.T.	1 hr. or H.T.	1 hr.	H.T.	H.T.	"	4 hr.	1 hr.	1 hr.
V 1-HR	4,400	6,600	8,800	8,800	"	1 story 50'	1 hr., <10' fm. p/l 2 hr., <5' fm. p/l 4 hr.	1 hr.	1 hr., <10' fm. p/l 2 hr., <5' fm. p/l 4 hr.	1 hr.	1 hr.	1 hr.[3]	1 hr.	1 hr.	"	2 hr.	1 hr.	1 hr.
V N	2,500	3,750	5,000	5,000	"	1 story 40'	<20' fm. p/l 1 hr., <10' fm. p/l 2 hr., <5' fm. p/l 4 hr.	None	<20' fm. p/l 1 hr., <10' fm. p/l 2 hr., <5' fm. p/l 4 hr.	None	None	1 hr.[3]	None	None	"	2 hr.	1 hr.[5]	None, ≥30 occupants 1 hr.

NOTES: See Tables 4.1 and 4.2 for exempt amounts of hazardous materials. For minimum distance from p/l, see Table 4.3.

1. The total combined area for multistory buildings may be 2× that shown, and the area of any single story must be ≤ that given above. **Figures given are maximums.** [505]

2. The maximum floor areas given "FOR 1 STORY BUILDINGS" may be increased where public ways or yards are ≥20' wide, according to the **rates** given here. **Figures given are maximums.** [506a]

3. Rated shafts are not required for:

   a. Openings between one floor only, not concealed w/in building const.

   b. In type V buildings, chutes and dumbwaiters <9 sq. ft. in cross-sectional area and lined w/gyp. bd. and sheet metal.

   c. Gas vents, factory-built chimneys, and piping through two floors max.

4. See Chapter 7, "Area Separations," page 80.

5. Corridors in non-rated buildings serving an occupant load <30 may be non-rated (excluding R-1 or any I occupancy). [3305g]

6. H-2 and H-3 occupancies containing hazardous materials in excess of those set forth in Table 7.1 must not exceed one story. [902j]

Table 4.6 H-3 Hazardous Occupancy

H-3	MAXIMUM ALLOWABLE SQ. FT.					Maximum Building Height [5D,507]	CONSTRUCTION (FIRE-RESISTIVE REQUIREMENTS IN HOURS)											
	For 1 Story Buildings[1] [5C]	2 Side Yards >20' Add 1¼% Per Foot Over 20'[2] [506a]	3 Side Yards >20' Add 2½% Per Foot Over 20'[2] [506a]	All Side Yards >20' Add 5% Per Foot Over 20'[2] [506a]	Additional Sq. Ft. If Sprinklered [506c]		Exterior Bearing Walls [9C]	Interior Bearing Walls [17A]	Exterior Non-bearing Walls [9C]	Structural Frame [17A]	Permanent Partitions [17A]	Shaft Enclosures [17A]	Floors/ Ceilings [17A]	Roofs/ Ceilings [17A]	Exterior Doors & Windows	Area Separation Walls[4] [505f]	Exit Corridors [3305g]	Exit Stairways [3306l]
Type I	Unlimited	Unlimited	Unlimited	Unlimited	None	Unlimited[6]	4 hr.	3 hr.	<40' fm. p/l 1 hr., <10' fm. p/l 2 hr., <5' fm. p/l 4 hr.	3 hr.	1 hr.	2 hr.	2 hr.	2 hr.	<20' fm. p/l ¾ hr., N.A. <5' fm. p/l	4 hr.	1 hr.	2 hr.
II F.R.	24,800	37,200	49,600	49,600	"	5 stories 160'[6]	4 hr.	2 hr.	"	2 hr.	1 hr.	2 hr.	2 hr.	1 hr.	"	4 hr.	1 hr.	2 hr.
II 1-HR	11,200	16,800	22,400	22,400	"	2 stories 65'[6]	1 hr., <10' fm. p/l 2 hr., <5' fm. p/l 4 hr.	1 hr.	1 hr., <10' fm. p/l 2 hr., <5' fm. p/l 4 hr.	1 hr.	1 hr.	1 hr.	1 hr.	1 hr.	"	2 hr.	1 hr.	1 hr.
II N	7,500	11,250	15,000	15,000	"	1 story 55'	<20' fm. p/l 1 hr., <10' fm. p/l 2 hr., <5' fm. p/l 4 hr.	None	<20' fm. p/l 1 hr., <10' fm. p/l 2 hr., <5' fm. p/l 4 hr.	None	None	1 hr.	None	None	"	2 hr.	1 hr.[5]	None, ≥30 occupants 1 hr.
III 1-HR	11,200	16,800	22,400	22,400	"	2 stories 65'[6]	4 hr.	1 hr.	1 hr., <10' fm. p/l 2 hr., <5' fm. p/l 4 hr.	1 hr.	1 hr.	1 hr.	1 hr.	1 hr.	"	4 hr.	1 hr.	1 hr.
III N	7,500	11,250	15,000	15,000	"	1 story 55'	4 hr.	None	<40' fm. p/l 1 hr., <10' fm. p/l 2 hr., <5' fm. p/l 4 hr.	None	None	1 hr.	None	None	"	4 hr.	1 hr.[5]	None, ≥30 occupants 1 hr.
IV H.T.	11,200	16,800	22,400	22,400	"	2 stories 65'[6]	4 hr.	1 hr.	"	1 hr. or H.T.	1 hr. or H.T.	1 hr.	H.T.	H.T.	"	4 hr.	1 hr.	1 hr.
V 1-HR	8,800	13,200	17,600	17,600	"	2 stories 50'[6]	1 hr., <10' fm. p/l 2 hr., <5' fm. p/l 4 hr.	1 hr.	1 hr., <10' fm. p/l 2 hr., <5' fm. p/l 4 hr.	1 hr.	1 hr.	1 hr.[3]	1 hr.	1 hr.	"	2 hr.	1 hr.	1 hr.
V N	5,100	7,650	10,200	10,200	"	1 story 40'	<20' fm. p/l 1 hr., <10' fm. p/l 2 hr., <5' fm. p/l 4 hr.	None	<20' fm. p/l 1 hr., <10' fm. p/l 2 hr., <5' fm. p/l 4 hr.	None	None	1 hr.[3]	None	None	"	2 hr.	1 hr.[5]	None, ≥30 occupants 1 hr.

1. The total combined area for multistory buildings may be 2× that shown, and the area of any single story must be ≤ that given above. **Figures given are maximums.** [505]

2. The maximum floor areas given "FOR 1 STORY BUILDINGS" may be increased where public ways or yards are ≥20' wide, according to the **rates** given here. **Figures given are maximums.** [506a]

3. Rated shafts are not required for:

   a. Openings between one floor only, not concealed w/in building const.

   b. In type V buildings, chutes and dumbwaiters <9 sq. ft. in cross-sectional area and lined w/gyp. bd. and sheet metal.

   c. Gas vents, factory-built chimneys, and piping through two floors max.

4. See Chapter 7, "Area Separations," page 80.

5. Corridors in non-rated buildings serving an occupant load <30 may be non-rated (excluding R-1 or any I occupancy). [3305g]

6. H-2 and H-3 occupancies containing hazardous materials in excess of those set forth in Table 7.1 must not exceed one story. [902j]

Table 4.7 H-4 Hazardous Occupancy

H-4	MAXIMUM ALLOWABLE SQ. FT.					Maximum Building Height[4] [5D,507]	CONSTRUCTION (FIRE-RESISTIVE REQUIREMENTS IN HOURS)											
	For 1 Story Buildings[1] [5C]	2 Side Yards >20' Add 1¼% Per Foot Over 20'[2] [506a]	3 Side Yards >20' Add 2½% Per Foot Over 20'[2] [506a]	All Side Yards >20' Add 5% Per Foot Over 20'[2] [506a]	Additional Sq. Ft. If Sprinklered[3,8] [506c]		Exterior Bearing Walls [9C]	Interior Bearing Walls [17A]	Exterior Non-bearing Walls [9C]	Structural Frame [17A]	Permanent Partitions [17A]	Shaft Enclosures [17A]	Floors/ Ceilings [17A]	Roofs/ Ceilings [17A]	Exterior Doors & Windows [9C]	Area Separation Walls[6] [505f]	Exit Corridors [3305g]	Exit Stairways [3306l]
Type I	Unlimited	Unlimited	Unlimited	Unlimited	1 story ×3 >1 story ×2	Unlimited	4 hr.	3 hr.	<40' fm. p/l 1 hr., <10' fm. p/l 2 hr., <5' fm. p/l 4 hr.	3 hr.	1 hr.	2 hr.	2 hr.	2 hr.	<20' fm. p/l 1¾ hr., N.A. <5' fm. p/l	4 hr.	1 hr.	2 hr.
II F.R.	24,800	37,200	49,600	49,600	"	5 stories 160'	4 hr.	2 hr.	"	2 hr.	1 hr.	2 hr.	2 hr.	1 hr.	"	4 hr.	1 hr.	2 hr.
II 1-HR	11,200	16,800	22,400	22,400	"	2 stories 65'	1 hr., <10' fm. p/l 2 hr., <5' fm. p/l 4 hr.	1 hr.	1 hr., <10' fm. p/l 2 hr., <5' fm. p/l 4 hr.	1 hr.	1 hr.	1 hr.	1 hr.	1 hr.	"	2 hr.	1 hr.	1 hr.
II N	7,500	11,250	15,000	15,000	"	1 story 55'	<20' fm. p/l 1 hr., <10' fm. p/l 2 hr., <5' fm. p/l 4 hr.	None	<20' fm. p/l 1 hr., <10' fm. p/l 2 hr., <5' fm. p/l 4 hr.	None	None	1 hr.	None	None	"	2 hr.	1 hr.[7]	None, ≥30 occupants 1 hr.
III 1-HR	11,200	16,800	22,400	22,400	"	2 stories 65'	4 hr.	1 hr.	1 hr., <10' fm. p/l 2 hr., <5' fm. p/l 4 hr.	1 hr.	1 hr.	1 hr.	1 hr.	1 hr.	"	4 hr.	1 hr.	1 hr.
III N	7,500	11,250	15,000	15,000	"	1 story 55'	4 hr.	None	<40' fm. p/l 1 hr., <10' fm. p/l 2 hr., <5' fm. p/l 4 hr.	None	None	1 hr.	None	None	"	4 hr.	1 hr.[7]	None, ≥30 occupants 1 hr.
IV H.T.	11,200	16,800	22,400	22,400	"	2 stories 65'	4 hr.	1 hr.	"	1 hr. or H.T.	1 hr. or H.T.	1 hr.	H.T.	H.T.	"	4 hr.	1 hr.	1 hr.
V 1-HR	8,800	13,200	17,600	17,600	"	2 stories 50'	1 hr., <10' fm. p/l 2 hr., <5' fm. p/l 4 hr.	1 hr.	1 hr., <10' fm. p/l 2 hr., <5' fm. p/l 4 hr.	1 hr.	1 hr.	1 hr.[5]	1 hr.	1 hr.	"	2 hr.	1 hr.	1 hr.
V N	5,100	7,650	10,200	10,200	"	1 story 40'	<20' fm. p/l 1 hr., <10' fm. p/l 2 hr., <5' fm. p/l 4 hr.	None	<20' fm. p/l 1 hr., <10' fm. p/l 2 hr., <5' fm. p/l 4 hr.	None	None	1 hr.[5]	None	None	"	2 hr.	1 hr.[7]	None, ≥30 occupants 1 hr.

1. The total combined area for multistory buildings may be 2× that shown, and the area of any single story must be ≤ that given above. **Figures given are maximums**. [505]

2. The maximum floor areas given "FOR 1 STORY BUILDINGS" may be increased where public ways or yards are ≥20' wide, according to the **rates** given here. **Figures given are maximums.** [506a]

3. The multiplying factor given here (a doubling or tripling of allowed sq. ft.) shall not apply when sprinklers are used to: increase the number of stories; substitute for 1-hr. const.; include atria; or use in an H-1, H-2, H-3, or H-7 occupancy. [506c] Also, see footnote 8.

4. These story limits may be increased by one story if the building is fully sprinklered, provided no other increase for sprinkling is used. [507] Also, see footnote 8.

5. Rated shafts are not required for:

   a. Openings between one floor only, not concealed w/in building const.

   b. In type V buildings, chutes and dumbwaiters <9 sq. ft. in cross-sectional area and lined w/gyp. bd. and sheet metal.

   c. Gas vents, factory-built chimneys, and piping through two floors max.

6. See Chapter 7, "Area Separations," page 80.

7. Corridors in non-rated buildings serving an occupant load <30 may be non-rated (excluding R-1 or any I occupancy). [3305g]

8. H-4 occupancies >3,000 sq. ft. are **required to be sprinklered**, and no increase for sprinkling is allowed. [3802]

Table 4.8   **H-5 Hazardous Occupancy**

H-5	MAXIMUM ALLOWABLE SQ. FT.					Maximum Building Height[4] [5D,507]	CONSTRUCTION (FIRE-RESISTIVE REQUIREMENTS IN HOURS)											
	For 1 Story Buildings[1] [5C]	2 Side Yards >20' Add 1¼% Per Foot Over 20'[2] [506a]	3 Side Yards >20' Add 2½% Per Foot Over 20'[2] [506a]	All Side Yards >20' Add 5% Per Foot Over 20'[2] [506a]	Additional Sq. Ft. If Sprinklered[3] [506c]		Exterior Bearing Walls [9C]	Interior Bearing Walls [17A]	Exterior Non-bearing Walls [9C]	Structural Frame [17A]	Permanent Partitions [17A]	Shaft Enclosures [17A]	Floors/ Ceilings [17A]	Roofs/ Ceilings [17A]	Exterior Doors & Windows	Area Separation Walls[6] [505f]	Exit Corridors [3305g]	Exit Stairways [3306l]
Type I	Unlimited	Unlimited	Unlimited	Unlimited	1 story×3 >1 story ×2[8]	Unlimited	4 hr.	3 hr.	None, <60' fm. p/l 1 hr., <40' fm. p/l 4 hr.	3 hr.	1 hr.	2 hr.	2 hr.	2 hr.	<60' fm. p/l 3/4 hr.	4 hr.	1 hr.	2 hr.
II F.R.	24,800	37,200	49,600	49,600	"	5 stories 160'	4 hr.	2 hr.	"	2 hr.	1 hr.	2 hr.	2 hr.	1 hr.	"	4 hr.	1 hr.	2 hr.
II 1-HR	11,200	16,800	22,400	22,400	"	2 stories 65'	1 hr.	1 hr.	None, <60' fm. p/l 1 hr.	1 hr.	1 hr.	1 hr.	1 hr.	1 hr.	"	2 hr.	1 hr.	1 hr.
II N	7,500	11,250	15,000	15,000	"	1 story 55'	None, <60' fm. p/l 1 hr.	None	"	None	None	1 hr.	None	None	"	2 hr.	1 hr.[7]	None, ≥30 occupants 1 hr.
III 1-HR	11,200	16,800	22,400	22,400	"	2 stories 65'	4 hr.	1 hr.	None, <60' fm. p/l 1 hr., <40' fm. p/l 4 hr.	1 hr.	1 hr.	1 hr.	1 hr.	1 hr.	"	4 hr.	1 hr.	1 hr.
III N	7,500	11,250	15,000	15,000	"	1 story 55'	4 hr.	None	"	None	None	1 hr.	None	None	"	4 hr.	1 hr.[7]	None, ≥30 occupants 1 hr.
IV H.T.	11,200	16,800	22,400	22,400	"	2 stories 65'	4 hr.	1 hr.	"	1 hr. or H.T.	1 hr. or H.T.	1 hr.	H.T.	H.T.	"	4 hr.	1 hr.	1 hr.
V 1-HR	8,800	13,200	17,600	17,600	"	2 stories 50'	1 hr.	1 hr.	1 hr.	1 hr.	1 hr.	1 hr.[5]	1 hr.	1 hr.	"	2 hr.	1 hr.	1 hr.
V N	5,100	7,650	10,200	10,200	"	1 story 40'	None, <60' fm. p/l 1 hr.	None	None, <60' fm. p/l 1 hr.	None	None	1 hr.[5]	None	None	"	2 hr.	1 hr.[7]	None, ≥30 occupants 1 hr.

1. The total combined area for multistory buildings may be 2× that shown, and the area of any single story must be ≤ that given above. **Figures given are maximums.** [505]

2. The maximum floor areas given "FOR 1 STORY BUILDINGS" may be increased where public ways or yards are ≥20' wide, according to the **rates** given here. **Figures given are maximums.** [506a]

3. The multiplying factor given here (a doubling or tripling of allowed sq. ft.) shall not apply when sprinklers are used to: increase the number of stories; substitute for 1-hr. const.; include atria; or use in an H-1, H-2, H-3, or H-7 occupancy. [506c]

4. These story limits may be increased by one story if the building is fully sprinklered, provided no other increase for sprinkling is used. [507]

5. Rated shafts are not required for:

   a. Openings between one floor only, not concealed w/in building const.

   b. In type V buildings, chutes and dumbwaiters <9 sq. ft. in cross-sectional area and lined w/gyp. bd. and sheet metal.

   c. Gas vents, factory-built chimneys, and piping through two floors max.

6. See Chapter 7, "Area Separations," page 80.

7. Corridors in non-rated buildings serving an occupant load <30 may be non-rated (excluding R-1 or any I occupancy). [3305g]

8. The area of any one- or two-story B or H-5 fully-sprinklered building with all yards ≥60' wide may be unlimited. [506b]

Table 4.9   **H-6 and H-7 Hazardous Occupancies**

H-6 & H-7	MAXIMUM ALLOWABLE SQ. FT.					Maximum Building Height [5D,507]	CONSTRUCTION (FIRE-RESISTIVE REQUIREMENTS IN HOURS)											
	For 1 Story Buildings[1] [5C]	2 Side Yards >20' Add 1 1/4% Per Foot Over 20'[2] [506a]	3 Side Yards >20' Add 2 1/2% Per Foot Over 20'[2] [506a]	All Side Yards >20' Add 5% Per Foot Over 20'[2] [506a]	Additional Sq. Ft. If Sprinklered [506c]		Exterior Bearing Walls [9C]	Interior Bearing Walls [17A]	Exterior Non-bearing Walls [9C]	Structural Frame [17A]	Permanent Partitions [17A]	Shaft Enclosures [17A]	Floors/ Ceilings [17A]	Roofs/ Ceilings [17A]	Exterior Doors & Windows [9C]	Area Separation Walls[4] [505f]	Exit Corridors [3305g]	Exit Stairways [3306l]
Type I	Unlimited	Unlimited	Unlimited	Unlimited	None	Unlimited feet 3 stories	4 hr.	3 hr.	<40' fm. p/l 1 hr., <10' fm. p/l 2 hr., <5' fm. p/l 4 hr.	3 hr.	1 hr.	2 hr.	2 hr.	2 hr.	<20' fm. p/l 3/4 hr., N.A. <5' fm. p/l	4 hr.	1 hr.	2 hr.
II F.R.	39,900	59,850	79,800	79,800	"	3 stories 160'	4 hr.	2 hr.	"	2 hr.	1 hr.	2 hr.	2 hr.	1 hr.	"	4 hr.	1 hr.	2 hr.
II 1-HR	18,000	27,000	36,000	36,000	"	3 stories 65'	1 hr., <10' fm. p/l 2 hr., <5' fm. p/l 4 hr.	1 hr.	1 hr., <10' fm. p/l 2 hr., <5' fm. p/l 4 hr.	1 hr.	1 hr.	1 hr.	1 hr.	1 hr.	"	2 hr.	1 hr.	1 hr.
II N	12,000	18,000	24,000	24,000	"	2 stories 55'	<20' fm. p/l 1 hr., <10' fm. p/l 2 hr., <5' fm. p/l 4 hr.	None	<20' fm. p/l 1 hr., <10' fm. p/l 2 hr., <5' fm. p/l 4 hr.	None	None	1 hr.	None	None	"	2 hr.	1 hr.[5]	None, ≥30 occupants 1 hr.
III 1-HR	18,000	27,000	36,000	36,000	"	3 stories 65'	4 hr.	1 hr.	1 hr., <10' fm. p/l 2 hr., <5' fm. p/l 4 hr.	1 hr.	1 hr.	1 hr.	1 hr.	1 hr.	"	4 hr.	1 hr.	1 hr.
III N	12,000	18,000	24,000	24,000	"	3 stories 55'	4 hr.	None	<40' fm. p/l 1 hr., <10' fm. p/l 2 hr., <5' fm. p/l 4 hr.	None	None	1 hr.	None	None	"	4 hr.	1 hr.[5]	None, ≥30 occupants 1 hr.
IV H.T.	18,000	27,000	36,000	36,000	"	3 stories 65'	4 hr.	1 hr.	"	1 hr. or H.T.	1 hr. or H.T.	1 hr.	H.T.	H.T.	"	4 hr.	1 hr.	1 hr.
V 1-HR	14,000	21,000	28,000	28,000	"	3 stories 50'	1 hr., <10' fm. p/l 2 hr., <5' fm. p/l 4 hr.	1 hr.	1 hr., <10' fm. p/l 2 hr., <5' fm. p/l 4 hr.	1 hr.	1 hr.	1 hr.[3]	1 hr.	1 hr.	"	2 hr.	1 hr.	1 hr.
V N	8,000	12,000	16,000	16,000	"	1 story 40'	<20' fm. p/l 1 hr., <10' fm. p/l 2 hr., <5' fm. p/l 4 hr.	None	<20' fm. p/l 1 hr., <10' fm. p/l 2 hr., <5' fm. p/l 4 hr.	None	None	1 hr.[3]	None	None	"	2 hr.	1 hr.[5]	None, ≥30 occupants 1 hr.

1. The total combined area for multistory buildings may be 2× that shown, and the area of any single story must be ≤ that given above. **Figures given are maximums.** [505]

2. The maximum floor areas given "FOR 1 STORY BUILDINGS" may be increased where public ways or yards are ≥20' wide, according to the **rates** given here. **Figures given are maximums.** [506a]

3. Rated shafts are not required for:

   a. Openings between one floor only, not concealed w/in building const.

   b. In type V buildings, chutes and dumbwaiters <9 sq. ft. in cross-sectional area and lined w/gyp. bd. and sheet metal.

   c. Gas vents, factory-built chimneys, and piping through two floors max.

   d. In H-6 occupancies, fabrication areas may have duct work and piping through max. two floors. [1706]

4. See Chapter 7, "Area Separations," page 80.

5. Corridors in non-rated buildings serving an occupant load <30 may be non-rated (excluding R-1 or any I occupancy). [3305g]

General Sanitation [510]

Water closet rooms: Must be separated from food preparation/ storage areas by a tight-fitting door.

Floors and walls in water closet rooms and showers: Must be of smooth, non-absorbant, hard finishes.

Walls must be so finished up to a minimum 48".

Shower walls must be so finished up to a minimum 70".

Floor base must be a minimum 5".

Light [905]

All occupied rooms must have either: Window opening(s) $\geq 1/10$ the floor area of the room.

or

Artificial light.

Ventilation [905]

All occupied rooms must have either: Openable window(s) with an area $\geq 1/20$ the floor area of the room.

or

Mechanical ventilation.

Toilet Rooms [905]

Toilet rooms must have ventilation by either: Openable window(s) ≥ 3 sq. ft.

or

Mechanical ventilation.

At least one lavatory and one water closet must be provided.

Separate facilities for each sex must be provided when the number of employees >4.

Barrier-free access: ≥ 1 of each sanitary fixture provided per floor must be accessible.

UPC recommended: (fixtures:persons)

Lab-Employee Use

Water Closets	Urinals	Lavs
1:1–15	1:50	1:40
2:16–35		
3:36–55		
>55 persons, add 1:40 persons		

Lab-Public Use

Water Closets	Lavs
1:1–15	1:1–15
2:16–35	2:16–35
3:36–55	3:36–60
4:56–80	4:61–90
5:81–110	5:91–125
6:111–150	>125 persons, add 1:45
>150 persons, add 1:40 persons	

UPC recommended:

Industrial/Warehouse

Water Closets	Lavs
1:1–10	1:10 persons up to
2:11–25	100 persons,
3:26–50	1:15 over 100 persons
4:51–75	
5:76–100	
>100 persons, add 1:30 addit. persons	

Drinking Fountains

Not required.

Barrier-free access: If provided, ≥1 fountain must be accessible to those in wheelchairs, and ≥1 fountain must be accessible to those who have difficulty bending.

UPC recommended: 1:75 persons.

H-4 Occupancies Handling Vehicles Operating Under Their Own Power [905]

Each workstation shall have an exhaust extension duct extending to the outside (the building official may waive this if the building has large, unobstructed openings).

Connected office and lounge space must be positive-pressurized.

5

I Occupancies

Table 5.1 I-1.1 and I-1.2 Institutional Occupancies

I-1.1 & I-1.2	MAXIMUM ALLOWABLE SQ. FT.					Maximum Building Height[4] [5D,507]	CONSTRUCTION (FIRE-RESISTIVE REQUIREMENTS IN HOURS)											
	For 1 Story Buildings[1] [5C]	2 Side Yards >20' Add 1¼% Per Foot Over 20'[2] [506a]	3 Side Yards >20' Add 2½% Per Foot Over 20'[2] [506a]	All Side Yards >20' Add 5% Per Foot Over 20'[2] [506a]	Additional Sq. Ft. If Sprinklered[3] [506c]		Exterior Bearing Walls [17A]	Interior Bearing Walls [17A]	Exterior Non-bearing Walls	Structural Frame [17A]	Permanent Partitions [17A]	Shaft Enclosures [17A]	Floors/ Ceilings [17A]	Roofs/ Ceilings [17A]	Exterior Doors & Windows	Area Separation Walls[7] [505f]	Exit Corridors [3305g]	Exit Stairways [3306l]
Type I	Unlimited	Unlimited	Unlimited	Unlimited	Unlimited	Unlimited	4 hr.	3 hr.	1 hr., <20' fm. p/l 2 hr., <5' fm. p/l 4 hr.[5]	3 hr.	1 hr.	2 hr.	2 hr.	2 hr.[8]	<20' fm. p/l 3/4 hr., N.A. <5' fm. p/l [1803b]	4 hr.	1 hr.	2 hr.
II F.R.	15,100	22,650	30,200	30,200	1 story ×3, >1 story ×2	3 stories 160'[9]	4 hr.	2 hr.	"	2 hr.	1 hr.	2 hr.	2 hr.	1 hr.[8]	" [1903b]	4 hr.	1 hr.	2 hr.
II 1-HR	6,800	10,200	13,600	13,600	"	1 story 65'[9]	1 hr., <5' fm. p/l 2 hr. [5A]	1 hr.	1 hr., <5' fm. p/l 2 hr. [5A][5]	1 hr.	1 hr.	1 hr.	1 hr.	1 hr.[8]	<10' fm. p/l 3/4 hr., N.A. <5' fm. p/l [5A]	2 hr.	1 hr.	1 hr.
II N[10]	13,500	20,250	27,000	27,000	None	1 story 55'	1 hr., <5' fm. p/l 2 hr. [5A]	None	1 hr., <5' fm. p/l 2 hr. [5A][5]	None	None	1 hr.	None	None	" [5A]	2 hr.	None, ≥10 occupants 1 hr.	1 hr.
III 1-HR	6,800	10,200	13,600	13,600	1 story ×3, >1 story ×2	1 story 65'	4 hr.	1 hr.	1 hr., <20' fm. p/l 2 hr., <5' fm. p/l 4 hr.[5]	1 hr.	1 hr.	1 hr.	1 hr.	1 hr.	<20' fm. p/l 3/4 hr., N.A. <5' fm. p/l [2003b]	4 hr.	1 hr.	1 hr.
IV H.T.	6,800	10,200	13,600	13,600	"	1 story 55'	4 hr.	1 hr.	"	1 hr. or H.T.	1 hr. or H.T.	1 hr.	H.T.	H.T.	" [2103b]	4 hr.	1 hr.	1 hr.
V 1-HR	5,200	7,800	10,400	10,400	"	2 stories 65'	1 hr., <5' fm. p/l 2 hr. [5A]	1 hr.	1 hr., <5' fm. p/l 2 hr. [5A]	1 hr.	1 hr.	1 hr.[6]	1 hr.	1 hr.	<10' fm. p/l 3/4 hr., N.A. <5' fm. p/l [5A]	2 hr.	1 hr.	1 hr.

(See Table 5.2, page 66 for required separation between I-1 Occupancies and specific use areas.)

1. The total combined area for multistory buildings may be 2× that shown, and the area of any single story must be ≤ that given above. **Figures given are maximums.** [505]

2. The maximum floor areas given "FOR 1 STORY BUILDINGS" may be increased where public ways or yards are ≥20' wide, according to the **rates** given here. **Figures given are maximums.** [506a]

3. The multiplying factor given here (a doubling or tripling of allowed sq. ft.) shall not apply when sprinklers are used to: increase the number of stories; substitute for 1-hr. const.; include atria; or use in an H-1, H-2, H-3, or H-7 occupancy. [506c]

4. These story limits may be increased by one story if the building is fully sprinklered, provided no other increase for sprinkling is used. [507]

5. Non-bearing walls fronting public ways or yards ≥40' wide may be non-rated, non-combust. [1803a, 1903a, 2003a, 2103a]

6. Rated shafts are not required, in type V buildings, for chutes and dumbwaiters <9 sq. ft. in cross-sectional area and lined w/gyp. bd. and sheet metal. [1706]

7. See Chapter 7, "Area Separations," page 80.

8. Roof const. (other than primary members) in type I, II-F.R., or II-1-hr. ≥25' above all floors/levels may be non-rated, non-combust. H.T. const. may be used if such building is only one story. [1806]

9. **Sprinklered** I-1.1 hospitals and nursing homes may be five stories max. when of type II-F.R., and three stories max. when of type II-1-hr. The area increase for side yards only applies when the number of stories is one less than that set forth here. [1002a]

10. **Sprinklered** I-1.1 hospitals and nursing homes may be housed within one-story type II-N buildings with max. area as set forth here. [1002a]

Table 5.2 **Required Separation of Specific Use Areas [10A]**

Description	Occupancy Separation
1. Employee locker rooms	None
2. Gift/retail shops	None
3. Handicraft shops	None
4. Kitchens	None
5. Laboratories which employ hazardous materials in quantities less than that which would cause classification as a Group H Occupancy	One hour
6. Laundries greater than 100 sq. ft.	One hour
7. Paint shops employing hazardous substances and materials in quantities less than that which would cause classification as a Group H Occupancy	One hour
8. Physical plant maintenance shop	One hour
9. Soiled linen room	One hour
10. Storage rooms 100 sq. ft. or less in area storing combustible material	None
11. Storage rooms more than 100 sq. ft. storing combustible material	One hour
12. Trash-collection rooms	One hour

Table 5.3 I-2 Institutional Occupancy

I-2	MAXIMUM ALLOWABLE SQ. FT.						CONSTRUCTION (FIRE-RESISTIVE REQUIREMENTS IN HOURS)											
I-2	For 1 Story Buildings[1] [5C]	2 Side Yards >20' Add 1¼% Per Foot Over 20'[2] [506a]	3 Side Yards >20' Add 2½% Per Foot Over 20'[2] [506a]	All Side Yards >20' Add 5% Per Foot Over 20'[2] [506a]	Additional Sq. Ft. If Sprinklered[3] [506c]	Maximum Building Height[4] [5D,507]	Exterior Bearing Walls [17A]	Interior Bearing Walls [17A]	Exterior Non-bearing Walls	Structural Frame [17A]	Permanent Partitions [17A]	Shaft Enclosures [17A]	Floors/ Ceilings [17A]	Roofs/ Ceilings [17A]	Exterior Doors & Windows	Area Separation Walls[7] [505f]	Exit Corridors [3305g]	Exit Stairways [3306l]
Type I	Unlimited	Unlimited	Unlimited	Unlimited	Unlimited	Unlimited	4 hr.	3 hr.	1 hr., <20' fm. p/l 2 hr., <5' fm. p/l 4 hr.[5]	3 hr.	1 hr.	2 hr.	2 hr.	2 hr.[8]	<20' fm. p/l ¾ hr., N.A. <5' fm. p/l [1803b]	4 hr.	1 hr.	2 hr.
II F.R.	15,100	22,650	30,200	30,200	1 story ×3, >1 story ×2	3 stories 160'	4 hr.	2 hr.	"	2 hr.	1 hr.	2 hr.	2 hr.	1 hr.[8]	" [1903b]	4 hr.	1 hr.	2 hr.
II 1-HR	6,800	10,200	13,600	13,600	"	2 stories 65'	1 hr. [5A]	1 hr.	1 hr. [5A][5]	1 hr.	1 hr.	1 hr.	1 hr.	1 hr.[8]	<10' fm. p/l ¾ hr., N.A. <5' fm. p/l [5A]	2 hr.	1 hr.	1 hr.
III 1-HR	6,800	10,200	13,600	13,600	"	2 stories 65'	4 hr.	1 hr.	1 hr., <20' fm. p/l 2 hr., <5' fm. p/l 4 hr.[5]	1 hr.	1 hr.	1 hr.	1 hr.	1 hr.	<20' fm. p/l ¾ hr., N.A. <5' fm. p/l [2003b]	4 hr.	1 hr.	1 hr.
IV H.T.	6,800	10,200	13,600	13,600	"	2 stories 65'	4 hr.	1 hr.	"	1 hr. or H.T.	1 hr. or H.T.	1 hr.	H.T.	H.T.	" [2103b]	4 hr.	1 hr.	1 hr.
V 1-HR	5,200	7,800	10,400	10,400	"	2 stories 55'	1 hr. [5A]	1 hr.	1 hr. [5A]	1 hr.	1 hr.	1 hr.[6]	1 hr.	1 hr.	<10' fm. p/l ¾ hr., N.A. <5' fm. p/l [5A]	2 hr.	1 hr.	1 hr.

1. The total combined area for multistory buildings may be 2× that shown, and the area of any single story must be ≤ that given above. **Figures given are maximums.** [505]

2. The maximum floor areas given "FOR 1 STORY BUILDINGS" may be increased where public ways or yards are ≥20' wide, according to the **rates** given here. **Figures given are maximums.** [506a]

3. The multiplying factor given here (a doubling or tripling of allowed sq. ft.) shall not apply when sprinklers are used to: increase the number of stories; substitute for 1-hr. const.; include atria; or use in an H-1, H-2, H-3, or H-7 occupancy. [506c]

4. These story limits may be increased by one story if the building is fully sprinklered, provided no other increase for sprinkling is used. [507]

5. Non-bearing walls fronting public ways or yards ≥40' wide may be non-rated, non-combust. [1803a, 1903a, 2003a, 2103a]

6. Rated shafts are not required, in type V buildings, for chutes and dumbwaiters <9 sq. ft. in cross-sectional area and lined w/gyp. bd. and sheet metal. [1706]

7. See Chapter 7, "Area Separations," page 80.

8. Roof const. (other than primary members) in type I, II-F.R., or II-1-hr. ≥25' above all floors/levels may be non-rated, non-combust. H.T. const. may be used if such building is only one story. [1806]

Table 5.4   I-3 Institutional Occupancy

I-3	MAXIMUM ALLOWABLE SQ. FT.					CONSTRUCTION (FIRE-RESISTIVE REQUIREMENTS IN HOURS)												
	For 1 Story Buildings[1] [5C]	2 Side Yards >20' Add 1¼% Per Foot Over 20'[2] [506a]	3 Side Yards >20' Add 2½% Per Foot Over 20'[2] [506a]	All Side Yards >20' Add 5% Per Foot Over 20'[2] [506a]	Additional Sq. Ft. If Sprinklered[3] [506c]	Maximum Building Height[4] [5D,507]	Exterior Bearing Walls [17A]	Interior Bearing Walls [17A]	Exterior Non-bearing Walls	Structural Frame [17A]	Permanent Partitions [17A]	Shaft Enclosures [17A]	Floors/ Ceilings [17A]	Roofs/ Ceilings [17A]	Exterior Doors & Windows	Area Separation Walls[7] [505f]	Exit Corridors [3305g]	Exit Stairways [3306I]
Type I	Unlimited	Unlimited	Unlimited	Unlimited	Unlimited	Unlimited	4 hr.	3 hr.	1 hr., <20' fm. p/l 2 hr., <5' fm. p/l 4 hr.[5]	3 hr.	1 hr.	2 hr.	2 hr.	2 hr.[8]	<20' fm. p/l ¾ hr., N.A. <5' fm. p/l [1803b]	4 hr.	1 hr.	2 hr.
II F.R.	15,100	22,650	30,200	30,200	1 story ×3, >1 story ×2	2 stories 160'	4 hr.	2 hr.	"	2 hr.	1 hr.	2 hr.	2 hr.	1 hr.[8]	" [1903b]	4 hr.	1 hr.	2 hr.
II 1-HR[9]	3,900	3,900	3,900	3,900	None	1 story 65'	1 hr., <5' fm. p/l 2 hr. [5A]	1 hr.	1 hr., <5' fm. p/l 2 hr. [5A]	1 hr.	1 hr.	1 hr.	1 hr.	1 hr.[8]	<10' fm. p/l ¾ hr., N.A. <5' fm. p/l [5A]	2 hr.	1 hr.	1 hr.
III 1-HR[9]	3,900	3,900	3,900	3,900	None	1 story 65'	4 hr.	1 hr.	1 hr., <20' fm. p/l 2 hr., <5' fm. p/l 4 hr.[5]	1 hr.	1 hr.	1 hr.	1 hr.	1 hr.	<20' fm. p/l ¾ hr., N.A. <5' fm. p/l [2003b]	4 hr.	1 hr.	1 hr.
V 1-HR[9]	3,900	3,900	3,900	3,900	None	1 story 50'	1 hr., <5' fm. p/l 2 hr. [5A]	1 hr.	1 hr., <5' fm. p/l 2 hr. [5A]	1 hr.	1 hr.	1 hr.[6]	1 hr.	1 hr.	<10' fm. p/l ¾ hr., N.A. <5' fm. p/l [5A]	2 hr.	1 hr.	1 hr.

1. The total combined area for multistory buildings may be 2× that shown, and the area of any single story must be ≤ that given above. **Figures given are maximums.** [505]

2. The maximum floor areas given "FOR 1 STORY BUILDINGS" may be increased where public ways or yards are ≥20' wide, according to the **rates** given here. **Figures given are maximums**. [506a]

3. The multiplying factor given here (a doubling or tripling of allowed sq. ft.) shall not apply when sprinklers are used to: increase the number of stories; substitute for 1-hr. const.; include atria; or use in an H-1, H-2, H-3, or H-7 occupancy. [506c]

4. These story limits may be increased by one story if the building is fully sprinklered, provided no other increase for sprinkling is used. [507]

5. Non-bearing walls fronting public ways or yards ≥40' wide may be non-rated, non-combust. [1803a, 1903a, 2003a, 2103a]

6. Rated shafts are not required, in type V buildings, for chutes and dumbwaiters <9 sq. ft. in cross-sectional area and lined w/gyp. bd. and sheet metal. [1706]

7. See Chapter 7, "Area Separations," page 80.

8. Roof const. (other than primary members) in type I, II-F.R., or II-1-hr. ≥25' above all floors/levels may be non-rated, non-combust. H.T. const. may be used if such building is only one story. [1806]

9. **One-story** I-3 occupancies of type II-F.R., II-1-hr., and V-1-hr. are allowed, providing their area ≤3,000 sq. ft. No increase in area or stories is allowed. Two-hr. separation walls may be used to separate adjoining areas of 3,000 sq. ft. [1002b] See Chapter 7, "Area Separations," page 80.

General Sanitation [510]

Water closet rooms: Must be separated from food preparation/storage areas by a tight-fitting door.

Floors and walls in water closet rooms and showers: Must be of smooth, non-absorbant, hard finishes w/ a min. 5" base.

Walls must be so finished up to a minimum 48".

Shower walls must be so finished up to a minimum 7".

Light [1005]

All occupied rooms must have either: Window opening(s) ≥1/10 the floor area of the room.

or

Artificial light.

Ventilation [1005]

All occupied rooms must have either: Openable window(s) with an area ≥1/20 the floor area of the room.

or

Mechanical ventilation.

Toilet Rooms [1005]

Toilet rooms must have ventilation by either: Openable window(s) ≥ 3 sq. ft.

or

Mechanical ventilation.

At least one lavatory for every two water closets for each sex must be provided.

Barrier-free access: ≥1 of each sanitary fixture provided per floor must be accessible. (See Barrier-free Access section, page 110 for patient rooms.)

UPC recommended: (fixtures:persons)

Hospitals-Employees

Water Closets	Urinals	Lavs
1:1–15	1:40	1:40
2:16–35		
3:36–55		
>55, add 1:40 addit. persons		

Hospitals-Waiting Room

Water Closets	Lavs
1:room	1:room

Hospitals-Patient Room

Water Closets	Lavs
1:room	1:room

Hospitals-Ward Room

Water Closets	Lavs
1:8 patients	1:10 patients

UPC recommended:

Penal Institutions Employee Use

Water Closets	Urinals	Lavs
1:1–15	1:50	1:40
2:16–35		
3:36–55		
>55, add 1:40 addit. persons		

Penal Institutions
Prisoner Use

Water Closets	Lavs
1:cell	1:cell

Other Institutions

Water Closets		Urinals	Lavs
Male	Female		
1:25	1:20	1:50	1:40

Other Institutions Employee Use

Water Closets	Urinals	Lavs
1:1–15	1:50	1:40
2:16–35		
3:36–55		
>55, add 1:40 addit. persons		

Drinking Fountains [1005]

At least one drinking fountain per floor must be provided.

Barrier-free access: ≥1 fountain per floor must be accessible to those in wheelchairs, and ≥1 fountain per floor must be accessible to those who have difficulty bending.

UPC recommended: 1:75 persons.

6

R Occupancies

Table 6.1 R-1 Residential Occupancy

R-1	For 1 Story Buildings[1] [5C]	2 Side Yards >20' Add 1¼% Per Foot Over 20'[2] [506a]	3 Side Yards >20' Add 2½% Per Foot Over 20'[2] [506a]	All Side Yards >20' Add 5% Per Foot Over 20'[2] [506a]	Additional Sq. Ft. If Sprinklered[3] [506c]	Maximum Building Height[4] [5D,507]	Exterior Bearing Walls [17A]	Interior Bearing Walls [17A]	Exterior Non-bearing Walls	Structural Frame [17A]	Permanent Partitions [17A]	Shaft Enclosures [17A]	Floors/Ceilings [17A]	Roofs/Ceilings [17A]	Exterior Doors & Windows	Area Separation Walls[10] [505f]	Exit Corridors [3305g]	Exit Stairways [3306I]
															MAXIMUM ALLOWABLE SQ. FT. + **CONSTRUCTION (FIRE-RESISTIVE REQUIREMENTS IN HOURS)**			
Type I	Unlimited	Unlimited	Unlimited	Unlimited	Unlimited	Unlimited	2 hr., <3' fm. p/l 4 hr.	3 hr.	1 hr., <20' fm. p/l 2 hr., <3' fm. p/l 4 hr.[5]	3 hr.	1 hr.	2 hr.	2 hr.	2 hr.[8]	<20' fm. p/l 1¾ hr., N.A. <5' fm. p/l [1803b]	4 hr.	1 hr.	2 hr.
II F.R.	29,000	44,850	59,800	59,800	1 story × 3, >1 story × 2	12 stories 160'	"	2 hr.	"	2 hr.	1 hr.	2 hr.	2 hr.	1 hr.[8]	" [1903b]	4 hr.	1 hr.	2 hr.
II 1-HR	13,500	20,250	27,000	27,000	"	4 stories 65'	1 hr. [5A]	1 hr.	1 hr. [5A]	1 hr.	1 hr.	1 hr.	1 hr.	1 hr.[8]	<10' fm. p/l 1¾ hr., N.A. <5' fm. p/l [5A]	2 hr.	1 hr.	1 hr., ≥ 4 stories 2 hr.
II N[9]	9,100	13,650	18,200	18,200	"	2 stories 55'	None, <5' fm. p/l 1 hr. [5A]	None[10]	None, <5' fm. p/l 1 hr.[5] [5A]	None	None[10]	1 hr.	None[10]	None	" [5A]	2 hr.	None, ≥10 occupants 1 hr.	"
III 1-HR	13,500	20,250	27,000	27,000	"	4 stories 65'	2 hr., <3' fm. p/l 4 hr.	1 hr.	1 hr., <20' fm. p/l 2 hr., <3' fm. p/l 4 hr.[5]	1 hr.	1 hr.	1 hr.	1 hr.	1 hr.	<20' fm. p/l 1¾ hr., N.A. <5' fm. p/l [2003b]	4 hr.	1 hr.	"
III N[9]	9,100	13,650	18,200	18,200	"	2 stories 55'	"	None[10]	"	None	None[10]	1 hr.	None[10]	None	" [2003b]	4 hr.	None, ≥10 occupants 1 hr.	"
IV H.T.	13,500	20,250	27,000	27,000	"	4 stories 65'	"	1 hr.	"	1 hr. or H.T.	1 hr. or H.T.	1 hr.	H.T.	H.T.	" [2103b]	4 hr.	1 hr.	"
V 1-HR	10,500	15,750	21,000	21,000	"	3 stories 50'	1 hr. [5A]	1 hr.	1 hr. [5A]	1 hr.	1 hr.	1 hr.[6]	1 hr.	1 hr.	<10' fm. p/l 1¾ hr., N.A. <5' fm. p/l [5A]	2 hr.	1 hr.	"
V N[9]	6,000	9,000	12,000	12,000	"	2 stories 40'	None, <5' fm. p/l 1 hr. [5A]	None[10]	None, <5' fm. p/l 1 hr. [5A]	None	None[10]	1 hr.[6]	None[10]	None	" [5A]	2 hr.	None, ≥10 occupants 1 hr.	"

1. The total combined area for multistory buildings may be 2× that shown, and the area of any single story must be ≤ that given above. **Figures given are maximums.** [505]

2. The maximum floor areas given "FOR 1 STORY BUILDINGS" may be increased where public ways or yards are ≥20' wide, according to the **rates** given here. **Figures given are maximums.** [506a]

3. The multiplying factor given here (a doubling or tripling of allowed sq. ft.) shall not apply when sprinklers are used to: increase the number of stories; substitute for 1-hr. const.; include atria; or use in an H-1, H-2, H-3, or H-7 occupancy. [506c]

4. These story limits may be increased by one story if the building is fully sprinklered, provided no other increase for sprinkling is used. [507]

5. Non-bearing walls fronting public ways or yards ≥40' wide may be non-rated, non-combust. [1803a, 1903a, 2003a, 2103a]

6. Rated shafts are not required for:

   a. Openings between one floor only, not concealed w/in building const.

   b. In type V buildings, chutes and dumbwaiters <9 sq. ft. in cross-sectional area and lined w/gyp. bd. and sheet metal.

   c. Gas vents, factory-built chimneys, and piping through two floors max. [1706]

7. See Chapter 7, "Area Separations," page 80.

8. Roof const. (other than primary members) in type I, II-F.R., or II-1-hr. ≥25' above all floors/levels may be non-rated, non-combust. H.T. const. may be used if such building is only one story. [1806]

9. R-1 occupancies >2 stories or with >3,000 sq. ft. of floor area above the first level **must be ≥1-hr. const.** [1202b]

10. Walls and floors **separating** individual dwelling units in the same building **must be ≥1-hr. const.** [1202b]

11. Stairways within individual dwelling units need not be enclosed. [3309]

Table 6.2 R-3 Residential Occupancy

R-3	MAXIMUM ALLOWABLE SQ. FT.					Maximum Building Height [1] [5D,507]	CONSTRUCTION (FIRE-RESISTIVE REQUIREMENTS IN HOURS)											
	For 1 Story Buildings [5C]	2 Side Yards >20' Add 1¼% Per Foot Over 20' [506a]	3 Side Yards >20' Add 2½% Per Foot Over 20' [506a]	All Side Yards >20' Add 5% Per Foot Over 20' [506a]	Additional Sq. Ft. If Sprinklered [506c]		Exterior Bearing Walls [17A]	Interior Bearing Walls [17A]	Exterior Non-bearing Walls	Structural Frame [17A]	Permanent Partitions [17A]	Shaft Enclosures [17A]	Floors/ Ceilings [17A]	Roofs/ Ceilings [17A]	Exterior Doors & Windows	Area Separation Walls [4] [505f]	Exit Corridors [3305g]	Exit Stairways [3306l][7]
Type I	Unlimited	Unlimited	Unlimited	Unlimited	Unlimited	Unlimited	2 hr., <3' fm. p/l 4 hr.	3 hr.	1 hr., <20' fm. p/l 2 hr., <3' fm. p/l 4 hr.[2]	3 hr.	1 hr.	2 hr.	2 hr.	2 hr.[5]	<20' fm. p/l 1¾ hr., N.A. <3' fm. p/l [1803b]	4 hr.	1 hr.	2 hr.
II F.R.	"	"	"	"	"	3 stories 160'	"	2 hr.	"	2 hr.	1 hr.	2 hr.	2 hr.	1 hr.[5]	" [1903b]	4 hr.	1 hr.	2 hr.
II 1-HR	"	"	"	"	"	3 stories 65'	1 hr. [5A]	1 hr.	1 hr. [5A]	1 hr.	1 hr.	1 hr.	1 hr.	1 hr.[5]	N.A. <3' fm. p/l [5A]	2 hr.	1 hr.	1 hr., ≥ 4 stories 2 hr.
II N	"	"	"	"	"	3 stories 55'	None, <3' fm. p/l 1 hr. [5A]	None[6]	None, <3' fm. p/l 1 hr.[2] [5A]	None	None[6]	1 hr.	None[6]	None	" [5A]	2 hr.	None, ≥30 occupants 1 hr.	"
III 1-HR	"	"	"	"	"	3 stories 65'	2 hr., <3' fm. p/l 4 hr.	1 hr.	1 hr., <20' fm. p/l 2 hr., <3' fm. p/l 4 hr.[2]	1 hr.	1 hr.	1 hr.	1 hr.	1 hr.	<20' fm. p/l 1¾ hr., N.A. <3' fm. p/l [2003b]	4 hr.	1 hr.	"
III N	"	"	"	"	"	3 stories 55'	"	None[6]	"	None	None[6]	1 hr.	None[6]	None	" [2003b]	4 hr.	None, ≥30 occupants 1 hr.	"
IV H.T.	"	"	"	"	"	3 stories 65'	"	1 hr.	"	1 hr. or H.T.	1 hr. or H.T.	1 hr.	H.T.	H.T.	" [2103b]	4 hr.	1 hr.	"
V 1-HR	"	"	"	"	"	3 stories 50'	1 hr. [5A]	1 hr.	1 hr.[5] [5A]	1 hr.	1 hr.	1 hr.[3]	1 hr.	1 hr.	N.A. <3' fm. p/l [5A]	2 hr.	1 hr.	"
V N	"	"	"	"	"	3 stories 40'	None, <3' fm. p/l 1 hr. [5A]	None[6]	None, <3' fm. p/l 1 hr. [5A]	None	None[6]	1 hr.[3]	None[6]	None	" [5A]	2 hr.	None, ≥30 occupants 1 hr.	"

1. These story limits may be increased by one story if the building is fully sprinklered, provided no other increase for sprinkling is used. [507]

2. Non-bearing walls fronting public ways or yards ≥40' wide may be non-rated, non-combust. [1803a, 1903a, 2003a, 2103a]

3. Rated shafts are not required for:

   a. Openings between one floor only, not concealed w/in building const.

   b. In type V buildings, chutes and dumbwaiters <9 sq. ft. in cross-sectional area and lined w/gyp. bd. and sheet metal.

   c. Gas vents, factory-built chimneys, and piping through two floors max. [1706]

4. See Chapter 7, "Area Separations," page 80.

5. Roof const. (other than primary members) in type I, II-F.R., or II-1-hr. ≥25' above all floors/levels may be non-rated, non-combust. H.T. const. may be used if such building is only one story. [1806]

6. Walls and floors **separating** individual dwelling units in the same building **must be ≥1-hr. const.** [1202b]

7. Stairways within individual dwelling units need not be enclosed. [3309]

Table 6.3   **R-4 Residential Occupancy**

R-4	MAXIMUM ALLOWABLE SQ. FT.					Maximum Building Height[4] [5D,507]	CONSTRUCTION (FIRE-RESISTIVE REQUIREMENTS IN HOURS)											
	For 1 Story Buildings[1] [5C]	2 Side Yards >20' Add 1¼% Per Foot Over 20'[2] [506a]	3 Side Yards >20' Add 2½% Per Foot Over 20'[2] [506a]	All Side Yards >20' Add 5% Per Foot Over 20'[2] [506a]	Additional Sq. Ft. If Sprinklered[3] [506c]		Exterior Bearing Walls [17A]	Interior Bearing Walls [17A]	Exterior Non-bearing Walls	Structural Frame [17A]	Permanent Partitions [17A]	Shaft Enclosures [17A]	Floors/ Ceilings [17A]	Roofs/ Ceilings [17A]	Exterior Doors & Windows	Area Separation Walls[7] [505f]	Exit Corridors [3305g]	Exit Stairways [3306l][11]
Type I	3,000	4,500	6,000	6,000	1 story×3 >1 story ×2	2 stories unlimited feet	2 hr., <3' fm. p/l 4 hr.	3 hr.	1 hr., <20' fm. p/l 2 hr., <3' fm. p/l 4 hr.[5]	3 hr.	1 hr.	2 hr.	2 hr.	2 hr.[8]	<20' fm. p/l 3/4 hr., N.A. <3' fm. p/l [1803b]	4 hr.	1 hr.	2 hr.
II F.R.	"	"	"	"	"	2 stories 160'	"	2 hr.	"	2 hr.	1 hr.	2 hr.	2 hr.	1 hr.[8]	" [1903b]	4 hr.	1 hr.	2 hr.
II 1-HR	"	"	"	"	"	2 stories 65'	1 hr. [5A]	1 hr.	1 hr. [5A]	1 hr.	1 hr.	1 hr.	1 hr.	1 hr.[8]	N.A. <3' fm. p/l [5A]	2 hr.	1 hr.	1 hr.
II N[10]	"	"	"	"	"	2 stories 55'	None, <3' fm. p/l 1 hr. [5A]	None[9]	None, <3' fm. p/l 1 hr.[5] [5A]	None	None[9]	1 hr.	None[9]	None	" [5A]	2 hr.	None, ≥10 occupants 1 hr.	"
III 1-HR	"	"	"	"	"	2 stories 65'	2 hr., <3' fm. p/l 4 hr.	1 hr.	1 hr., <20' fm. p/l 2 hr., <3' fm. p/l 4 hr.[5]	1 hr.	1 hr.	1 hr.	1 hr.	1 hr.	<20' fm. p/l 3/4 hr., N.A. <3' fm. p/l [2003b]	4 hr.	1 hr.	"
III N[10]	"	"	"	"	"	2 stories 55'	"	None[9]	"	None	None[9]	1 hr.	None[9]	None	" [2003b]	4 hr.	None, ≥10 occupants 1 hr.	"
IV H.T.	"	"	"	"	"	2 stories 65'	"	1 hr.	"	1 hr. or H.T.	1 hr. or H.T.	1 hr.	H.T.	H.T.	" [2103b]	4 hr.	1 hr.	"
V 1-HR	"	"	"	"	"	2 stories 50'	1 hr. [5A]	1 hr.	1 hr. [5A]	1 hr.	1 hr.	1 hr.[6]	1 hr.	1 hr.	N.A. <3' fm. p/l [5A]	2 hr.	1 hr.	"
V N[11]	"	"	"	"	"	2 stories 40'	None, <3' fm. p/l 1 hr. [5A]	None[9]	None, <3' fm. p/l 1 hr. [5A]	None	None[9]	1 hr.[6]	None[9]	None	" [5A]	2 hr.	None, ≥10 occupants 1 hr.	"

1. The total combined area for multistory buildings may be 2× that shown, and the area of any single story must be ≤ that given above. **Figures given are maximums.** [505]

2. The maximum floor areas given "FOR 1 STORY BUILDINGS" may be increased where public ways or yards are ≥20' wide, according to the **rates** given here. **Figures given are maximums.** [506a]

3. The multiplying factor given here (a doubling or tripling of allowed sq. ft.) shall not apply when sprinklers are used to: increase the number of stories; substitute for 1-hr. const.; include atria; or use in an H-1, H-2, H-3, or H-7 occupancy. [506c]

4. These story limits may be increased by one story if the building is fully sprinklered, provided no other increase for sprinkling is used. [507]

5. Non-bearing walls fronting public ways or yards ≥40' wide may be non-rated, non-combust. [1803a, 1903a, 2003a, 2103a]

6. Rated shafts are not required for:

   a. Openings between one floor only, not concealed w/in building const.

   b. In type V buildings, chutes and dumbwaiters <9 sq. ft. in cross-sectional area and lined w/gyp. bd. and sheet metal.

   c. Gas vents, factory-built chimneys, and piping through two floors max. [1706]

7. See Chapter 7, "Area Separations," page 80.

8. Roof const. (other than primary members) in type I, II-F.R., or II-1-hr. ≥25' above all floors/levels may be non-rated, non-combust. H.T. const. may be used if such building is only one story. [1806]

9. Walls and floors **separating** individual dwelling units in the same building **must be ≥1-hr. const.** [1202b]

10. R-4 buildings with >3,000 sq. ft. of floor area above the first level **must be ≥1-hr. const.** [UBC Appendix, chap 12]

11. Stairs within individual dwelling units need not be enclosed.

General Sanitation [510]

Water closet rooms: Must be separated from food preparation/storage areas by a tight-fitting door.

Floors and walls in water closet rooms and showers: Must be of smooth, non-absorbent, hard finishes.

Walls must be so finished up to a minimum 48".

Shower walls must be so finished up to a minimum 70".

Floor base must be a minimum 5".

Light [1205]

All guest rooms, dorms, and habitable rooms with ≥ 10 sq. ft. within a dwelling unit must have: Windows with an area $\geq 1/10$ of the floor area.

Ventilation [1205]

All guest rooms, dorms, and habitable rooms within a dwelling unit must have either: Openable window(s) with an area $\geq 1/20$ the floor area of the room (window(s) min. 5 sq. ft.).

or

Mechanical ventilation.

All bathrooms, water closet rooms, and laundry rooms must have either: Openable window(s) with an area $\geq 1/20$ the floor area (window(s) min. 1½ sq. ft.)

or

Mechanical ventilation,

Note: In determining light and ventilation, any room may be considered a portion of an adjoining room when $\geq 1/2$ of the area of the common wall is open.

Toilet Rooms [1205]

At least one water closet must be provided.

Every hotel or subdivision thereof where both sexes are accommodated must have: At least two separate toilet facilities, each with at least one water closet.

Every floor of hotels must have at least one water closet for each sex at a rate of 1:10 guests.

Every dwelling unit must have: A bathroom with a water closet, a sink, and a bathtub or shower.

A kitchen with a sink.

All of the aforementioned must be provided with hot and cold running water.

Barrier-free access: For number of accessible units in multiple dwelling unit buildings, see Chapter 9.

Private, individual dwelling units do not require barrier-free access.

UPC recommended:

Dormitories Staff Use

Water Closets	Urinals	Lavs
1:1–15	1:50	1:40
2:16–35		
3:36–55		
>55, add 1:40 addit. persons		

Dormitories Resident Use

Water Closets		Urinals	Lavs
Male	Female		
1:10 >10, add 1:25 addit. males	1:6 >6, add 1:20 addit. females	1:25 >150, add 1:50 addit. males	1:12>12, add 1:20 addit.males, and 1:15 addit. females

Dwellings

Water Closets	Lavs
1:dwelling	1:dwelling

7

Building Separations

Definition [5B]

If occupancies are mixed within one building, each part of the building comprising a distinct occupancy must be separated from other occupancies. (See Figure 7.1.)

Table 7.1 lists the fire-resistive separations required between occupancies, in hours.

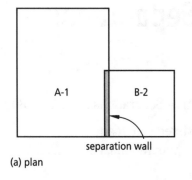

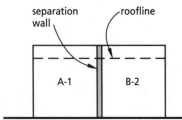

(a) plan

(b) elevation

Figure 7.1
Mixed Occupancies.

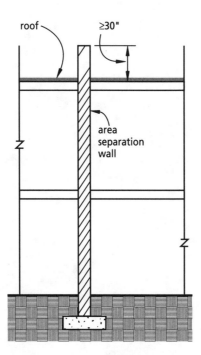

Figure 7.2
Separation Wall Extension.

Exceptions:

The following need not be separated from their primary uses:

Assembly rooms ≤750 sq. ft.

Admin. & clerical areas ≤25 percent of the floor area (excluding H-2 and H-3 occupancies).

Kitchens serving dining areas.

Gift shops and admin. areas ≤10 percent of the floor area in R-1 occupancies.

Spray booths in H or B occupancies (constructed per Fire Code).

Separations/Fire Ratings

1-hr. 1-hr. walls and opening assemblies.

2-hr. 2-hr. walls, 1½-hr. opening assemblies.

3-hr. 3-hr. walls, 3-hr. opening assemblies with ≤25 percent of wall length being (an) opening(s) **and** ≤120 sq. ft. of opening(s).

4-hr. 4-hr. walls, no openings.

Definition [505f]

Each portion of a building separated by area separation walls (construction conforming to the requirements described herein) may be considered a separate building, for purposes of max. sq. ft., max. building height, and fire-resistive requirements.

Table 7.1 **Required Separation in Buildings of Mixed Occupancy (in Hours) [5B]**

	A-1	A-2	A-2.1	A-3	A-4	B-1	B-2	B-3	B-4	E	H-1	H-2	H-3	H-4-5	H-6-7	I	M	R-1	R-3
A-1		N	N	N	N	4	3	3	3	N		4	4	4	4	3	1	1	1
A-2	N		N	N	N	3	1	1	1	N		4	4	4	4	3	1	1	1
A-2.1	N	N		N	N	3	1	1	1	N		4	4	4	4	3	1	1	1
A-3	N	N	N		N	3	N	1	1	N		4	4	4	3	2	1	1	1
A-4	N	N	N	N		3	1	1	1	N		4	4	4	4	3	1	1	1
B-1	4	3	3	3	3		1	1	1	3		2	1	1	1	4	1	3	1
B-2	3	1	1	N	1	1		1	1	1		2	1	1	1	2	1	1	1
B-3	3	1	1	1	1	1	1		1	1		2	1	1	1	3	1	1	1
B-4	3	1	1	1	1	1	1	1		1		2	1	1	1	4	N	1	1
E	N	N	N	N	N	3	1	1	1			4	4	4	3	1	1	1	1
H-1	Not Permitted in Mixed Occupancies																		
H-2	4	4	4	4	4	2	2	2	2	4			1	1	2	4	1	4	4
H-3	4	4	4	4	4	1	1	1	1	4		1		1	1	4	1	3	3
H-4-5	4	4	4	4	4	1	1	1	1	4		1	1		1	4	1	3	3
H-6-7	4	4	4	3	4	1	1	1	1	3		2	1	1		4	3	4	4
I	3	3	3	2	3	4	2	3	4	1		4	4	4	4		1	1	1
M	1	1	1	1	1	1	1	1	N	1		1	1	1	3	1		1	1
R-1	1	1	1	1	1	3	1	1	1	1		4	3	3	4	1	1		N
R-3	1	1	1	1	1	1	1	1	1	1		4	3	3	4	1	1	N	

1. 4-hr. separations between B-3 open parking garages and A-1 or I occupancies may be reduced to 3-hr. if no repair or fueling is done.

2. 3-hr. separations between B-3 open parking garages and R-1 occupancies may be reduced to 2-hr. if no repair or fueling is done.

3. 3-hr. separations between B-3 open parking garages and A-2, A-2.1, A-3, A-4, and E occupancies may be reduced to 2-hr. if no repair or fueling is done.

4. Mixed occupancies are not allowed with H-1 occupancies.

Fire Resistance

Walls: (See occupancy chart, "Area Separations" column.)

Openings:

In 2-hr. separation walls: Opening assemblies must be ≥1½-hr.

In 4-hr. separation walls: Opening assemblies must be ≥3-hr.

Extensions of area separation walls

Above roof: Area separation walls must extend from the foundation to a point ≥30" above the roof.

(See Figure 7.2.)

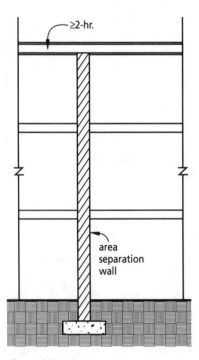

Figure 7.3
Separation Wall Extension Exception.

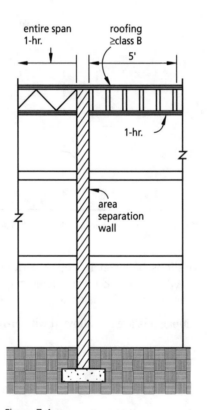

Figure 7.4
Separation Wall Extension Exception.

Exceptions:

1. Area separation walls may end at the underside of roof sheathing/deck/slab if the roof/ceiling assembly is ≥2-hr.

(See Figure 7.3.)

2. 2-hr. separation walls may end at the underside of roof sheathing/deck/slab where:

   a. Roof/ceiling framing that is parallel to the separation wall is 1-hr. for ≥5' on each side of the separation wall.

and

   b. Roof/ceiling framing that is perpendicular to the separation wall is 1-hr. for its entire span.

and

   c. No openings in the roof occur within 5' of the separation wall.

and

   d. Roofing is ≥Class B.

(See Figure 7.4.)

3. 2-hr. area separation walls may end at the underside of non-combustible roof sheathing/deck/slab where:

   a. No openings in the roof occur within 5' of the separation wall.

and

   b. Roofing is ≥Class B.

Beyond exterior walls: Area separation walls must extend to the outer edges of all horizontal projecting elements such as:

— Balconies

— Overhangs

— Canopies

— Other architectural projections

Exception: When the horizontal projecting element does not contain any concealed spaces, the separation wall may end at the exterior wall.

Parapet Faces

Parapets of area separation walls must be non-combustible for the uppermost 18", including flashing and coping.

Buildings of Different Heights

Where an area separation wall separates areas of a building with different heights, the separation wall may end at a point 30" above the lower roof level, provided the exterior wall is ≥1-hr. for a height ≥10' above the lower roof.

(See Figure 7.5.)

Exception: The area separation wall may end at the underside of roof sheathing/deck/slab where:

1. Roof framing members that are parallel to the separation wall are ≥1-hr. for a width ≥10' alongside the separation wall at the lower roof.

and

2. Roof framing members that are perpendicular to the separation wall are ≥1-hr. for their entire span.

and

3. No openings in the lower roof occur within 10' of the separation wall.

(See Figure 7.6.)

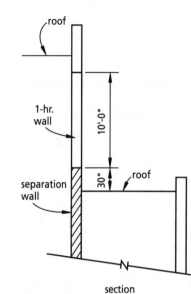

Figure 7.5
Separation Wall Between Buildings of Different Heights.

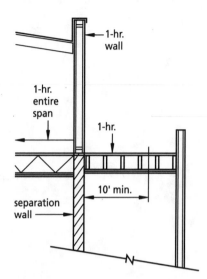

Figure 7.6
Separation Extension Exception.

Part 2
Exiting

8

Exiting

Introduction

Chapter structure

This chapter derives its information primarily from the 1991 UBC, incorporating pertinent barrier-free access guidelines where applicable (complete barrier-free access requirements can be found in the Chapter 9). Information is presented from the general to the specific, beginning with exiting requirements, such as number of exits and exit width, and ending with specific information regarding assembly uses.

Use vs. occupancy

Exiting requirements are derived from the **area/building use**, not occupancy. It is possible to have different uses (see Table 8.1) within one occupancy (such as an office, stock room, and retail sales space all within a B-2 occupancy). Buildings with different occupancies will often, but not always, have different uses. Each use has an "occupant load factor" that is divided into the *area for the use* to calculate the occupant load. This occupant load is then used to determine exiting requirements. (For a complete description of occupant load, see Table 8.1, page 89.) Again, occupant load and thus most exiting requirements are a resultant of *use*.

Effective use

This chapter can be used to set parameters prior to design, or to check a design or existing building for compliance with the major exiting requirements. In either case, a knowledge of **building area** and **area use** is necessary.

Quantifiable exiting requirements comprise a large part of this chapter and are best checked and recorded in the "Exiting" portion of the checklist. Spatial and relationship descriptive requirements such as arrangement of exits and exits through adjoining rooms are graphically presented within this chapter for quick reference and easy comparison.

Occupant Load [3302]

The first step in exiting research is calculating the area for each use. (See Table 8.1.) These areas will be used to calculate the building occupant load. Each use area having a differ-

ent occupant load factor (as listed in Table 8.1) must be calculated for occupant load separately. To derive a total building occupant load, add the area occupant loads together. Occupant load is used to determine exiting requirements such as exit width, number of exits, corridor width, and stair width. It is also essential in determining construction requirements for exits in some occupancies and types of construction.

Occupant load formula: (See Table 8.1.)

$$\text{Gross floor area (assigned to that use)} = \frac{\text{Occupant load}}{\substack{\text{Occupant load factor} \\ \text{(from Table 8.1.)}}}$$

For mixed occupancies: The occupant load is determined by calculating each use area separately, then adding the occupant load figures to derive the total building occupant load.

For buildings/areas with multiple uses in the same area: The occupant load is derived from the use which gives the largest number of people.

For areas with fixed seating: The occupant load is the number of fixed seats.

For areas with benches or pews: The occupant load is based on one person: each 18" of bench/pew length.

For booths in dining areas: The occupant load is based on one person: each 24" of booth length.

Number of Exits Required [3303a]

Every building or portion thereof must have at least one exit, ≥2 exits if required by Table 8.1, and additional exits as described here:

Basements and occupied roofs: Must have exits as required for any other story.

Exception: Occupied roofs on R-3 buildings may have only one exit if the occupied area is <500 sq. ft. and is located no higher than immediately above the second story.

Second stories: Must have at least two exits when the occupant load ≥10.

Floors above the second story and basements: Must have at least two exits.

Table 8.1 Minimum Egress Requirements [33A]

Use	Minimum of Two Exits Other Than Elevators are Required Where Number of Occupants is at Least	Occupant Load Factor[1] (sq. ft.)	Use	Minimum of Two Exits Other Than Elevators are Required Where Number of Occupants is at Least	Occupant Load Factor[1] (sq. ft.)
1. Aircraft hangars (no repair)	10	500	11. Dwellings	10	300
2. Auction rooms	30	7	12. Exercising rooms	50	50
3. Assembly areas, concentrated use (without fixed seats) Auditoriums Churches and chapels Dance floors Lobby accessory to assembly occupancy Lodge rooms Reviewing stands Stadiums	50	7	13. Garage, parking	30	200
			14. Hospitals and sanitariums— Nursing homes Sleeping rooms Treatment rooms Health-care center	6 10 10	80 80 80
Waiting Area	50	3	15. Hotels and apartments	10	200
4. Assembly areas, less-concentrated use Conference rooms Dining rooms Drinking establishments Exhibit rooms Gymnasiums Lounges Stages	50	15	16. Kitchen—commercial	30	200
			17. Library reading room	50	50
			18. Locker rooms	30	50
			19. Malls	—	—
			20. Manufacturing areas	30	200
			21. Mechanical equipment room	30	300
5. Bowling alley (assume no occupant load for bowling lanes)	50	4 [2]	22. Nurseries for children (day care)	7	35
			23. Offices	30	100
6. Children's homes and homes for the aged	6	80	24. School shops and vocational rooms	50	50
7. Classrooms	50	20	25. Skating rinks	50	50 on the skating area; 15 on the deck
8. Congregate residences (accommodating 10 or less persons and having an area of 3,000 square feet or less)	10	300			
Congregate residences (accommodating more than 10 persons or having an area of more than 3,000 square feet)	10	200	26. Storage and stock rooms	30	300
			27. Stores—retail sales rooms	50	30
			28. Swimming pools	50	50 for the pool area; 15 on the deck
9. Courtrooms	50	40	29. Warehouses	30	500
10. Dormitories	10	50	30. All others	50	100

[1] This table shall not be used to determine working space requirements per person.
[2] Occupant load based on five persons for each alley, including 15 feet of runway.

Reproduced from the 1991 edition of the *Uniform Building Code*, copyright © 1991, with the permission of the publishers, the International Conference of Building Officials.

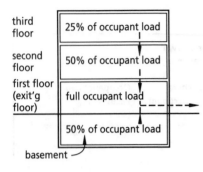

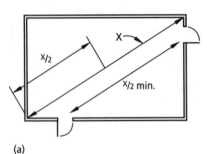

(a)

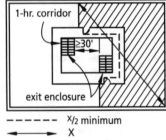

(b)

Figure 8.2
Arrangement of Exits.

Figure 8.1
Multiple Story Buildings, Number of Exits Calculation.

Exceptions:

1. ≥2 dwelling units on the second story or basement may have only one common exit if their total occupant load <11.

2. Only one exit is required from the second story or basement within an individual dwelling unit (except as required by Table 8.1).

3. When the third floor within an individual dwelling unit is ≤500 sq. ft., only one exit is required.

4. Floors and basements used exclusively for service of the building may have only one exit. This exception does not include storage rooms, laundry rooms, maintenance offices, and similar uses w/ areas >300 sq. ft.

Stories with an occupant load of 501–1,000: Must have at least three exits.

Stories with an occupant load >1,000: Must have at least four exits.

Number of exits required from multiple story buildings: May be determined by using the occupant load of the story under consideration + the percentage of the occupant loads of floors which exit onto the level under consideration as follows:

50% of the occupant load in the first adjacent story above (and below when a story below exits through the level under consideration).

and

25% of the occupant load in the story immediately beyond the first adjacent story.

(See Figure 8.1.)

Exit Width [3303b]

The total minimum required width (in inches) of exits must be provided according to the following formula:

Total occupant load served by the exit	×	0.02 *or* 0.03 (stairs)	=	Total exit width in inches

The width of exits must be divided approximately equally among these exits.

Note: To maintain **barrier-free access**, exit width must be ≥**36"**.

Arrangement of Exits [3303c]

If only two exits are required: Exits must be placed a distance apart ≥ ½ **the diagonal distance** of the building/area served by the exits, measured in a straight line.

(See Figure 8.2a.)

Exception: When exit enclosures are provided as part of the exiting system and are interconnected by a rated corridor, exit separations may be measured along the line of travel within the exit corridor. Enclosure walls must be ≥ 30' apart.

(See Figure 8.2b.)

If three or more exits are required: At least two exits must be placed ≥½ the diagonal distance of the building/area served by the exits.

Additional exits must be placed so that if one exit becomes blocked, the others will be available.

Exits Through Adjoining Rooms [3303e]

Rooms may have **one exit** through an adjoining or intervening room which provides a direct and obvious route to an exit, exit corridor, or exit enclosure.

(See Figure 8.3.)

In other than dwelling units, exits must not pass through kitchens, toilet rooms, closets, store rooms, or mechanical rooms.

Foyers, lobbies, and reception rooms constructed as required for corridors are *not* considered intervening rooms.

Exception: Rooms within dwelling units may exit through >1 room.

Adjoining rooms and cumulative occupant load: Adjoining rooms with a **cumulative occupant load** ≤**10** may exit through >1 intervening room.

(See Figure 8.4.)

Horizontal Exit [3308]

A horizontal exit is an exit from one building into another building on approximately the same level.

or

An exit through or around a 2-hr. occupancy separation.

A horizontal exit may not be used as the only exit, but may be used as one exit when two or more are required.

Maximum number of horizontal exits: A maximum of ½ of the exits may be horizontal exits.

Openings in horizontal exits: Openings must be ≥1½-hr.

Discharge areas: A horizontal exit must lead to a floor area with the capacity for an occupant load ≥ the occupants served by the horizontal exit. The capacity must be calculated according to the following:

3 sq. ft./occupant served.

In **I-1.1 occupancies,** the capacity must be calculated per:

15 sq. ft./ambulatory occupant.

and

30 sq. ft./non-ambulatory occupant.

Smokeproof Enclosures [3310]

Smokeproof enclosures are **vestibules** (either open-air or mechanically ventilated) **leading to a continuous stairway** from the building's highest point to its lowest, exiting into an exit passageway or out into a public way or yard.

When required: Smokeproof enclosures are required in buildings with occupied floors **>75'** above the lowest level of fire department access.

Exceptions:

1. Sprinklered buildings with enclosed stairways with positive pressure and barometric dampered relief openings at the stairway top connected to a smoke detector do not require smokeproof enclosures. (See UBC section 3310 for explicit ventilation requirements.)

2. Open parking garages do not require smokeproof enclosures.

Vestibule size: (See Figure 8.5.)

Smokeproof enclosure construction:

Walls	2-hr.
Floors/ceilings	2-hr.
Opening assemblies	1½-hr.

Grade-level barrier: A barrier must occur at grade level to prevent persons exiting from continuing on below grade (if basement levels occur).

Vestibule ceiling smoketrap: The vestibule ceiling must be ≥ **20"** above the door opening into the vestibule, to act as a smoke/heat trap.

Open-air vestibules: For a vestibule to be considered "open-air," it must have ≥**16 sq. ft. open** in a wall facing a **public way or yard** ≥ **20' wide**.

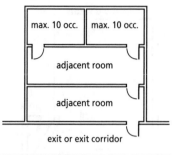

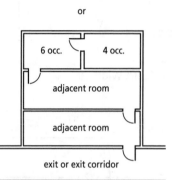

Figure 8.4
Adjoining Rooms and Cumulative Occupancy Load.

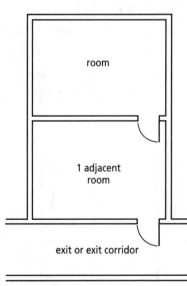

NOTE: max. distance remains unchanged.

Figure 8.3
Exit Through Adjoining Room.

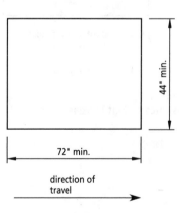

Figure 8.5
Smokeproof Enclosure Vestibule Size.

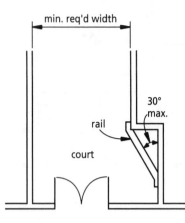

min. req'd width

30° max.

rail

court

Figure 8.6
Exit Court Width.

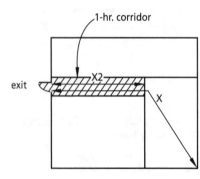

1-hr. corridor

exit

X2

X

X = max. total dist. to exit, with increase

X2 = increase distance

Figure 8.7
Distance to Exit Increase.

Exit Courts [3311]

Exit courts are yards or courts providing access to a public way for ≥1 required exit.

Width: Exit court width must be ≥ **the required exit width**, computed for the total number of people the court serves.

When an exit court width is reduced, a **guardrail ≥36" high** at an angle ≤30 degrees must be provided.

(See Figure 8.6.)

Height: Exit courts must have a clear height ≥**7'-0"**.

Construction: If the exit court serves ≥**10 people** or is <10'-0" wide, it must have:

Walls	≥1-hr.
Openings	≥3/4-hr. assembly

These fire resistance construction requirements apply to walls and openings in the exit court ≤10'-0" **above the court floor.**

Exit Passageways [3312]

Exit passageways are enclosed exits connecting a required exit with a public way or yard.

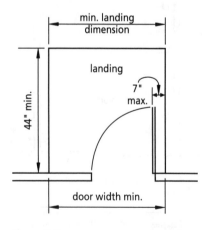

min. landing dimension

landing

7" max.

44" min.

door width min.

Figure 8.8
Exit Door Landing.

Construction:

Walls/floors/ceilings	≥1-hr.
Openings	3/4-hr. assembly

Distance to exits stair width, corridor width: (See Table 8.2.)

Exit Doors [3304]

Exit doors must conform to the following specifications:

Width	≥36"
Height	≥6'-8"
Single leaf max. width	≤48"
Landings	(See Figure 8.8 and Chapter 9.)
Landings at stairs	(See "Stairs," page 94.)

Doors in the fully open position must not reduce a required dimension (such as landings) by >**7"**.

(See Figure 8.9.)

When a landing serves an occupant load ≥**50**, doors in any position must not reduce a required dimension by >**1/2**.

(See Figure 8.10.)

Exception: In **R-3** occupancies and within individual dwelling units within an **R-1** occupancy, landings may be ≥**36"**.

Door swing: Exit doors must swing in the direction of travel.

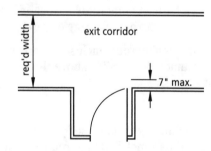

req'd width

exit corridor

7" max.

Figure 8.9
Doors Swinging Into Corridors.

Table 8.2 Minimum Exiting Requirements

Group	Min. Stair and Landing Width[1] [3306b]	Min. Corridor Width[1] [3305b]	Maximum Distance to Exits [2] [3303d]		
			If Bldg. is not Sprinklered	If Bldg. is Sprinklered	If w/in 1-Hr. Corridor [6]
A-1	44"	44"	150'	200'	Add 100'
A-2, A-2.1	<50 occ. 36"	<50 occ. 36"	"	"	"
A-3	≥50 occ. 44"	≥50 occ. 44"			"
A-4					
B (ALL)	"	"	" 7	" 3	"
E (ALL) [8]	<50 occ. 36"	"4	≤ 2 stories 175'	225'	No addit. dist.
	≥50 occ. 44"		>2 stories 150'		
	≥100 occ. 60"				
H-1	<50 occ. 36"	<50 occ. 36"	75'	No addit. dist.	"
H-2	≥50 occ. 44"	≥50 occ. 44"			
H-3					
H-4	"	"	150'	200'	Add 100'
H-5					
H-6	"	"	100'	No addit. dist.	No addit. dist.
H-7					
I (ALL)	"	44" 5 [3320]	150'	200'	Add 100'
R-1	"	<50 occ. 36"	150'	200'	Add 100'
R-3		≥50 occ. 44"			
R-4	36"	36"	75'	100'	Add 100'

1. See also, "Exit Width" page 94. Stairways adjacent to an area for evacuation assistance [3104] must be ≥48" wide between handrails.

2. Distance to exits is the maximum distance of travel from any point to an exterior door, horizontal exit, exit passageway, or an enclosed stairway. [3303d]

3. In a one-story B-4 fully sprinklered building classified as an airplane hangar, factory, or warehouse, this distance may be increased to 400'. [3303d]

4. The width of a corridor in E-1 occupancies shall be the minimum "exit width" +24", but not less than 6'-0". [3318e]

5. Corridors serving any area housing non-ambulatory persons shall be ≥8'-0" wide. See state codes. [3320c]

6. The maximum distance to exits may be increased up to the figure given in this column when the increased travel distance is entirely within a 1-hr. corridor. This 1-hr. corridor must be the last (closest to exit) portion of the travel distance. [3303d]

(See Figure 8.7.)

7. In a B-3 open parking garage, the maximum distance to exits in a non-sprinkled building may be increased to 250'. [3303d]

8. In E occupancies, every room with an occupant load >300 must have one of its exits open into a separate exit system (one with complete atmospheric separation). [3318b]

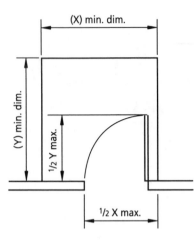

Figure 8.10
Exit Doors Serving ≥50 Occupants.

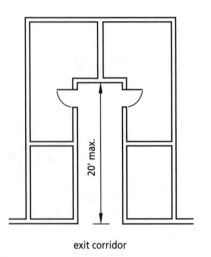

Figure 8.11
Dead End Corridors.

Exit Corridors [3305]

Exit corridors must conform to the following specifications:

Width   (See Table 8.2.)

Height   ≥7'-0"

Construction   (See occupancy charts, "Corridors" column.)

Dead-end corridors: Corridors with only one direction of exit must be ≤ **20'-0" long**.

(See Figure 8.8 and Chapter 9.)

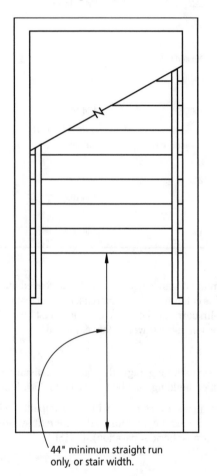

44" minimum straight run only, or stair width.

Figure 8.12
Exit Stair Landing.

Stairways [3306]

Stairways must conform to the following specifications:

Width   (See Table 8.2.)

Verticle distance between landings   ≤12'-0"

Landings   (See Figure 8.12.)

Exception: Stairs serving an unoccupied roof are exempt from these provisions.

Rise and run   (See Figure 8.13.)

Riser height may not vary <³/8" between the largest and the smallest, within a flight.

Exceptions:

1. Private stairways serving >**10 occupants** and stairways to unoccupied roofs may have a rise ≤8" and a run ≥9".

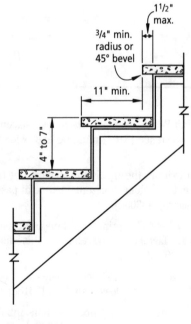

Figure 8.13
Exit Stair Rise and Run.

2. Where a bottom or top riser adjoins a **sloping** public way, the riser may be reduced along the slope, with the variation in height of riser ≤**3" for every 36" of stairway width**.

(See Figure 8.14.)

Winding And Circular Stairways [3306d, 3306e]

Curved or circular (not spiral) stairways are allowed in all occupancies.

Winding stairways are allowed in only R-1 and R-3 occupancies:

(See Figure 8.15 for tread run requirements.)

Spiral Stairways [3306F]

Spiral stairways are allowed only in **R-3** occupancies and private stairways within dwelling units in **R-1** occupancies.

Spiral stairways may be used as one required exit when the area they serve is ≤**400 sq. ft.**

Tread runs (See Figure 8.16.)

Headroom ≥6'-6"

Tread rise ≤9 1/2"

Handrails [3306i]

Spacing: All stairways must have handrails on each side.

Stairways >**88"** wide must have at least one intermediate handrail placed at approximate midpoint across the stairway width.

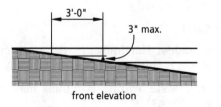

Figure 8.14
Stairways Adjoining Sloping Public Way.

Exceptions:

1. Stairways <**44"** wide **or** in individual dwelling units in **R-1** and **R-3** occupancies may have only one handrail.

2. Private stairways <**31"** wide may have only one handrail.

3. Stairways having <**4** risers in individual dwelling units may have no handrails.

Height: (See Figure 8.17.)

Return: At least one handrail must have returns that extend as follows:

(See Figure 8.18.)

Ramps
(See Chapter 9.)

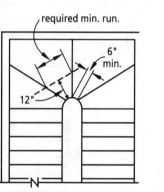

(a) winding stairs

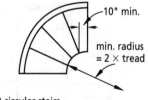

(b) circular stairs

Figure 8.15
Minimum Tread Run.

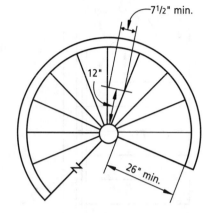

spiral stairs

Figure 8.16
Minimum Tread Run.

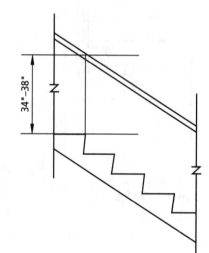

Figure 8.17
Handrail Height.

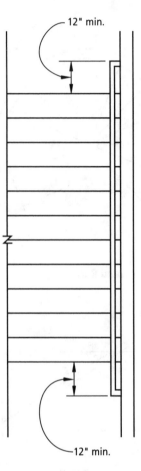

12" min.

12" min.

Figure 8.18
Handrail Return.

Aisles [3315]
Width in buildings without fixed seats:

In areas serving employees only:

≥24".

or

If greater, the "exit width" required by the number of employees served.

In areas in B-2 or assembly occupancies:

≥36" where obstructions are on only one side.

and

≥44" where obstructions are on both sides.

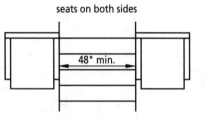

seats on both sides

48" min.

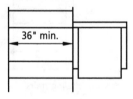

seats on 1 side

36" min.

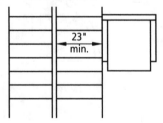

handrail in aisle

23" min.

Figure 8.19
Aisle Width in Stepped Aisles.

Width in occupancies with fixed seats:

In stepped aisles:

(slopes >1:8)

Clear aisle width (in inches) must be ≥ the occupant load served × 0.3.

and

When the **rise** of steps >7", the aisle clear width must be increased by 1¼" for every 100 occupants served for each ¼" the rise is >7".

Step **runs** must be ≥11".

In ramped aisles:

(slopes ≤1:8)

Clear aisle width (in inches) must be ≥ the occupant load served × 0.2.

Width in assembly rooms with fixed seats in rows:

In stepped aisles:

≥48" in aisles with seats on both sides.

≥36" in aisles with seats on one side.

≥23" between a stair handrail and seats, when the aisle is subdivided by a handrail

(See Figure 8.19.)

In ramped aisles:

≥42" in aisles with seats on both sides.

≥36" in aisles with seats on one side

≥23" between a ramp handrail and seats, when the aisle serves ≤5 rows on one side.

(See Figure 8.20.)

Handrails in aisles: Handrails in aisles must comply with barrier-free access requirements (See Chapter 9.)

Projection into aisle width: Handrails may project into required aisle width ≤**3½"**.

Handrail gap: Handrails within aisles must be discontinuous, with gaps at intervals of ≤**5 rows.**

(See Figure 8.21.)

Exception: Handrails may be omitted in ramped aisles with a slope <1:8, if fixed seats are on both sides.

Aisle termination: Aisles must terminate at either:

A cross aisle.

or

A foyer.

or

A doorway.

or

A vomitory.

Dead-end aisles: Aisles with only one direction of exit must be ≤20' deep.

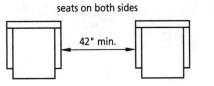

seats on both sides

42" min.

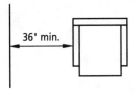

seats on 1 side

36" min.

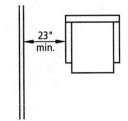

handrail in aisle

23" min.

Figure 8.20
Aisle Width in Ramped Aisles.

Seat Spacing (Fixed Seating) [3316]

Seats in rows with ≤14 seats: Clear width between edge of seat and seat back in next row must be ≥12".

(See Figure 8.22.)

When seats are self-rising, the clear width may be measured when the seats are raised.

Seats in rows with >14 seats:

Rows of seats with aisles or doorways on both ends must have:

≤**100** seats per row.

12" clear width must be increased by 0.3" for each seat >14 seats.

Required clear width need not exceed 22".

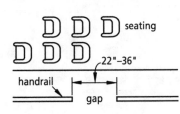

handrails

12"

34"–38"

(a) elevation

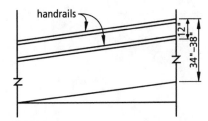

seating

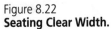

22"–36"

handrail

gap

seating

(b) plan

Figure 8.21
Aisle Handrail.

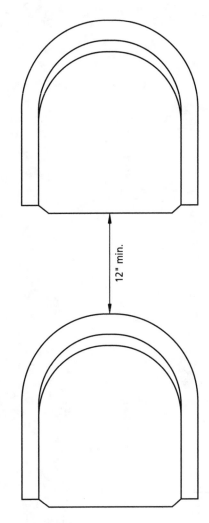

12" min.

Figure 8.22
Seating Clear Width.

Rows of seats with aisles or doorways on only one end:

12" clear width must be increased by **0.6"** for each seat **>7 seats**.

Required clear width need not exceed **22"**.

The max. travel distance to a point where the occupant has a choice of ≥2 directions of exit is **30'**.

"A" Occupancy Special Exiting Requirements [3317]

Side exits: Auditoriums must have exits on each side large enough to accommodate ⅓ the total occupant load.

Side exits must be accessible from a cross-aisle and lead to an exit, exit passageway, exit stair, public way, or yard.

Balcony exits: The number and distribution of balcony exits must be calculated as for other exits.

Balcony exits must be accessible from a cross-aisle.

Exits from one balcony: Exits from one balcony must lead directly to an exit stairway or ramp.

Exits from multiple balconies: When there is >1 balcony, exits must lead directly to an exterior (or enclosed) stairway or ramp.

Balconies with an occupant load >10: Such balconies must have ≥ **2 exits**.

Part 3
Barrier-Free Access

9

Barrier-Free Access

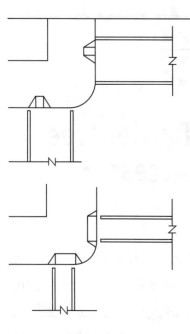

Figure 9.1
Curb Ramp at Marked Crossing.

Introduction

This chapter derives its information primarily from the Federal Americans with Disabilities Act of 1990, which prescribes national standards for access, and took effect in January of 1992. Generally speaking, the act mandates that all new construction and alteration to existing structures/sites, with the exception of single-family residences, must provide a barrier-free accessible route within the site, into and within the building, and to all spaces and features required to be accessible.

The intent of this chapter is to reorganize, outline, and graphically present general barrier-free design guidelines from the ADA and other sources, for use in schematic and preliminary design.

Chapter structure

This chapter is organized much in the same way a person would access a site and building, from the public domain to and into the building, and from general to specific. This arrangement leads the user through an accessible route, into the site, from parking, into the building, and to all required spaces and features.

Effective use

Like Chapter 8, this chapter can be used to either set parameters prior to design or to check a design or existing structure/site for compliance with accessibility requirements. Since most of the information presented in this chapter is graphic, it is most effectively used during design, redesign, or programming.

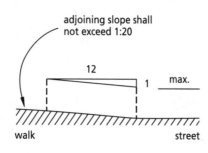

Figure 9.2
Curb Ramp Slope.

Illustration sources

Figures 9.3, 9.4, 9.5, 9.10, 9.13, 9.15, 9.16, 9.17, 9.18, 9.21, 9.22 through 9.26, 9.28, 9.29, 9.30, 9.31, and 9.33 through 9.40 were derived, with permission, from the American National Standard Institute's standard A117.1-1986. This is the same document that serves as a reference for the Federal Americans with Disabilities Act of 1990. Figures 9.6, 9.7, 9.8, 9.9, 9.11, 9.12, and 9.20 were derived from the *California State Accessibility Standards, Interpretive Manual*, 1989, with permission from the Office of the State Architect, California.

Curb Ramps

Curb ramps are required anywhere an accessible route crosses a curb, including:

—All intersections.

—Barrier-free parking stalls.

(See Figures 9.1 through 9.6.)

Parking

The following number of barrier-free parking spaces are required:

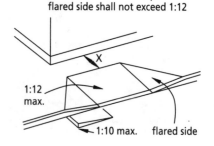

Figure 9.3
Curb Ramp.

This material is reproduced with permission from American National Standard A117.1-1986, copyright 1986 by the American National Standards Institute. Copies of this standard may be purchased from the American National Standards Institute at 11 West 42nd Street, New York, New York 10036.

Total # of spaces	# of barrier-free spaces required
1–25	1
26–50	2
51–75	3
76–100	4
101–150	5
151–200	6
201–300	7
301–400	8
401–500	9
501–1,000	2% of total spaces
>1,000	20 spaces + 1 space for every 100 spaces, or fraction thereof over 1,000

Barrier-free parking stalls must be located as near as possible to the primary building entrance.

Barrier-free parking spaces must be located/arranged to permit the user to exit the vehicle and enter the building without traveling behind another parked car, other than his/her own.

(See Figures 9.6 and 9.7 for typical layout.)

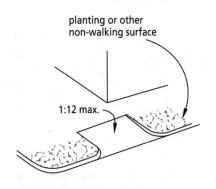

Figure 9.4
Curb Ramp.
This material is reproduced with permission from American National Standard A117.1-1986, copyright 1986 by the American National Standards Institute. Copies of this standard may be purchased from the American National Standards Institute at 11 West 42nd Street, New York, New York 10036.

Van access: 1:8 accessible parking spaces, but not less than one space, must be designated and designed for van access.

(See Figures 9.6 and 9.7.)

Passenger loading zones: If passenger loading zones are provided, at least one must be barrier-free.

(See Figure 9.8.)

Walks and Sidewalks

All public walks and sidewalks providing an accessible route must maintain barrier-free accessibility. Private walks and sidewalks are required to be accessible if they lead to buildings or facilities required to be accessible.

Width: Accessible walks must be ≥36" wide.

Passing space: If the accessible route is <60", then a **60"×60"** passing space is required at intervals ≤**200'**.

(See Figure 9.9.)

Protruding objects: Protruding objects must not reduce the required width of an accessible route.

Objects whose leading edges are >27" and <80" above the ground: Must not protrude >4" into an accessible route.

Objects whose leading edges are ≤27" above the ground: May protrude any amount.

Freestanding objects mounted on posts or pylons: May overhang ≤12" from 27"–80" above the ground.

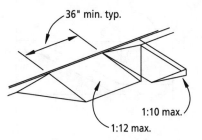

Figure 9.5
Built-Up Curb Ramp.
This material is reproduced with permission from American National Standard A117.1-1986, copyright 1986 by the American National Standards Institute. Copies of this standard may be purchased from the American National Standards Institute at 11 West 42nd Street, New York, New York 10036.

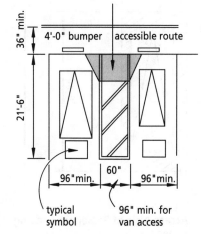

Figure 9.6
Handicap Spaces, Double Type.
Reproduced with permission from the California State Accessibility Standards Interpretive Manual, 1989, with permission from the Office of the State Architect, California.

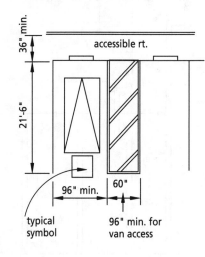

Figure 9.7
Handicap Spaces, Single Type.
Reproduced with permission from the California State Accessibility Standards Interpretive Manual, 1989, with permission from the Office of the State Architect, California.

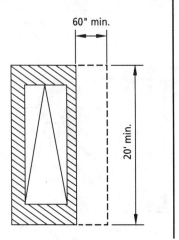

Figure 9.8
Access Aisle at Passenger Loading Zones.
Reproduced with permission from the California State Accessibility Standards Interpretive Manual, 1989, with permission from the Office of the State Architect, California.

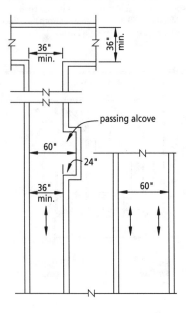

Figure 9.9
Route Width.
Reproduced with permission from the California State Accessibility Standards Interpretive Manual, 1989, with permission from the Office of the State Architect, California.

Headroom: Accessible routes must have ≥**80**" clear headroom.

Level Changes

A change in grade level may be made by the following:

Up to ¼"   No slope needed.

¼"–½"   1:2 bevel is permitted.

>½"   A ramp must be provided.

(See Figure 9.10.)

Ramps: Any path of travel shall be considered a ramp if its slope is >**1' rise in 20' of run** and its total rise >½".

Slope: ≤**1:12**

Width: ≥**36**", or as required for exits.

(See Figures 9.11 and 9.12.)

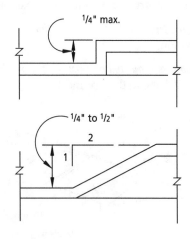

Figure 9.10
Changes in Level.
This material is reproduced with permission from American National Standard A117.1-1986, copyright 1986 by the American National Standards Institute. Copies of this standard may be purchased from the American National Standards Institute at 11 West 42nd Street, New York, New York 10036.

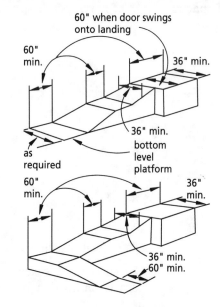

Figure 9.11
Typical Ramp Configurations.
Reproduced with permission from the California State Accessibility Standards Interpretive Manual, 1989, with permission from the Office of the State Architect, California.

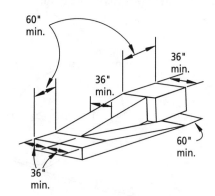

NOTE: For additional dimensions and notes, see Figure 9.11.

Figure 9.12
Typical Ramp Configurations.
Reproduced with permission from the California State Accessibility Standards Interpretive Manual, 1989, with permission from the Office of the State Architect, California.

Handrails

Handrails are required whenever the change in grade/floor level is ≥**6"**, or the horizontal projection is ≥72".

Exception: Curb ramps do not require handrails.

(See Figure 9.13.)

Building Entrances/Doors

All primary entrances and required exits to buildings and facilities must maintain barrier-free access.

Revolving doors may not be used as a required entrance or exit.

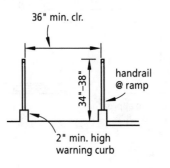

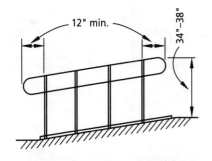

Door width and depth: (See Figure 9.14.)

Space at doors: (See Figures 9.15 through 9.19.)

Interior Access Route/Corridors

Every interior access route/corridor must be ≥**36" wide**, and as required by exiting requirements.

Passing space: If an accessible route is <60" wide, a 60"× 60" passing space must be provided at intervals ≤**200'**.

(See Figure 9.20.)

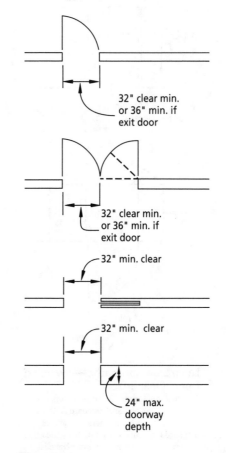

Figure 9.14
Door Width.

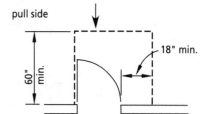

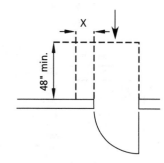

NOTE: X=12" if door has both a closer & latch.

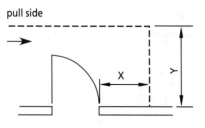

pull side

NOTE: X=36" min. if Y=60";
X=42" min. if Y=54".

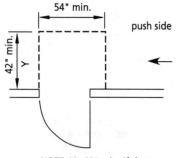

54" min.

42" min.

push side

Y

NOTE: Y=48" min. if door
has both a latch & closer.

Figure 9.16
Hinge Side Approaches—Swinging Doors Clear Space.

Turns in route ≥90 degrees: Where such turns occur, the following clear space requirements must be met:

(See Figure 9.21.)

Alcoves: Maneuvering space for accessible alcoves in accessible routes must meet the following criteria:

(See Figures 9.22 and 9.23.)

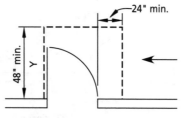

24" min.

48" min.

Y

NOTE: Y = 54" min. if
door has closer.

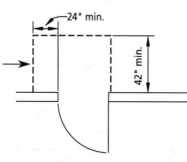

24" min.

42" min.

NOTE: Y = 48" min. if
door has closer.

Figure 9.17
Latch Side Approaches—Swinging Doors Clear Space.

Interior Facilities

All facilities required to be accessible must be along an accessible route.

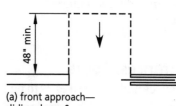

48" min.

(a) front approach—
sliding doors &
folding doors.

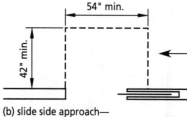

54" min.

42" min.

(b) slide side approach—
sliding doors &
folding doors.

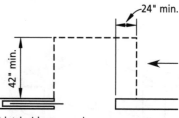

24" min.

42" min.

(c) latch side approach—
sliding doors &
folding doors
clear space.

Figure 9.18
Latch Side Approaches—Sliding Doors and Folding Doors Clear Space.

Toilet rooms:

1. If single water closet rooms are provided, ≥**1 per floor** must have barrier-free access.

(See Figures 9.24 and 9.25.)

2. Where multiple stalls are provided, ≥**1 stall per floor** must have barrier-free access.

(See Figures 9.25 and 9.26.)

Additional sanitary facilities: Where additional sanitary facilities are required/provided, such as **urinals, lavatories, showers, or bathtubs,** ≥**1 per floor** must have barrier-free access.

(See Figures 9.27 through 9.32.)

Drinking fountains: If only one location of drinking fountain(s) per floor is provided, it must be accessible to those who use wheelchairs (see Figures 9.33 and 9.34), and **one fountain must also be provided at standard height (rim at approx. 40")** for those who have difficulty bending.

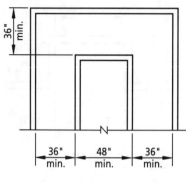

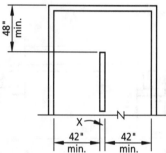

NOTE: dimensions
apply when X < 48".

Figure 9.21
Turns in Route.
This material is reproduced with permission from American National Standard A117.1-1986, copyright 1986 by the American National Standards Institute. Copies of this standard may be purchased from the American National Standards Institute at 11 West 42nd Street, New York, New York 10036.

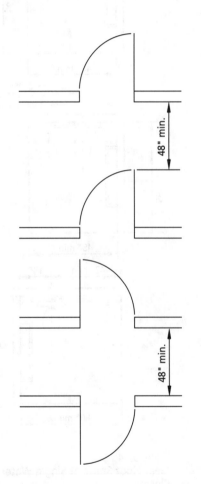

Figure 9.19
Clear Space Between Doors.

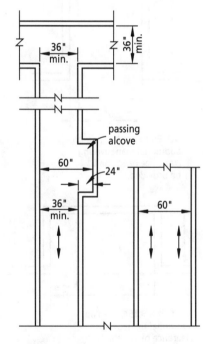

Figure 9.20
Route Width.
Reproduced with permission from the California State Accessibility Standards Interpretive Manual, 1989, with permission from the Office of the State Architect, California.

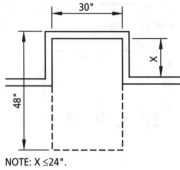

NOTE: X ≤24".

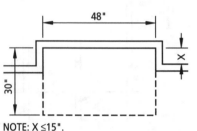

NOTE: X ≤15".

Figure 9.22
Clear Floor Space in Alcoves.
This material is reproduced with permission from American National Standard A117.1-1986, copyright 1986 by the American National Standards Institute. Copies of this standard may be purchased from the American National Standards Institute at 11 West 42nd Street, New York, New York 10036.

If >1 location of fountain(s) is provided, 50 percent of these fountains must be accessible to those who use wheelchairs.

Telephones: If public telephones are provided, ≥1 telephone must be accessible to those who use wheelchairs. (See Figures 9.35 and 9.36.)

If a bank or banks (two or more adjacent telephones) are provided, ≥1 **telephone per bank** must be accessible to those who use wheelchairs.

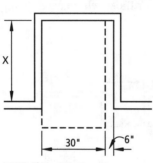

NOTE: if X > 24", then an additional maneuvering clearance of 6" shall be provided.

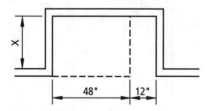

NOTE: if X > 15", then an additional maneuvering clearance of 12" shall be provided as shown.

Figure 9.23
Alcove Clear Space.
This material is reproduced with permission from American National Standard A117.1-1986, copyright 1986 by the American National Standards Institute. Copies of this standard may be purchased from the American National Standards Institute at 11 West 42nd Street, New York, New York 10036.

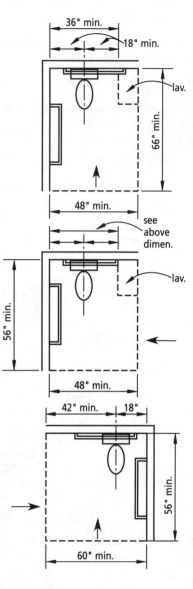

Figure 9.24
Clear Floor Space at Single Water Closets.
This material is reproduced with permission from American National Standard A117.1-1986, copyright 1986 by the American National Standards Institute. Copies of this standard may be purchased from the American National Standards Institute at 11 West 42nd Street, New York, New York 10036.

Volume control: All accessible telephones must have a volume control.

Elevators: Buildings ≤**3 stories** must be provided with elevators serving all floors/levels (including mezzanines) that have barrier-free access.

(See Figure 9.37.)

Exception: Buildings with <3,000 sq. ft. per floor are not required to have accessible elevators, unless the building is a shopping center or a medical/medical office building.

Seat Spacing/Fixed Seating

Non-assembly use: In facilities providing fixed or built-in seating and tables (restaurants, bars, study carrels, student laboratories and classrooms) ≥**5 percent**, but not <1, must be wheelchair accessible and along an accessible route.

(See Figure 9.38.)

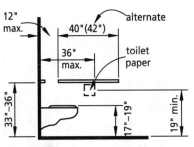

(a) side walls

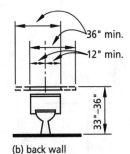

(b) back wall

Figure 9.25
Grab Bars.

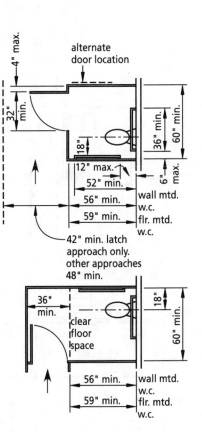

Figure 9.26
Stall Arrangements at Multiple Stalls.

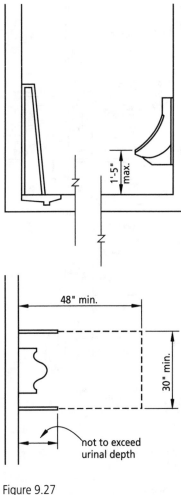

Figure 9.27
Urinals.

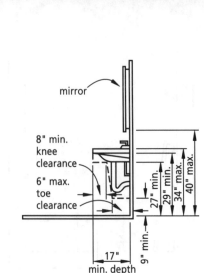

8" min. knee clearance

6" max. toe clearance

17" min. depth

(a) lavatory clearances

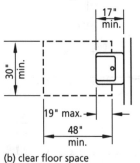

17" min.

30" min.

19" max.

48" min.

(b) clear floor space @ lavatory

Figure 9.28
Lavatories.
This material is reproduced with permission from American National Standard A117.1-1986, copyright 1986 by the American National Standards Institute. Copies of this standard may be purchased from the American National Standards Institute at 11 West 42nd Street, New York, New York 10036.

Assembly use: In assembly occupancies with fixed seating, wheelchair accessible seating must be provided as follows:

Capacity of Seating	Min. Number of Wheelchair Locations
4–25	1
26–50	2
51–300	4
301–500	6
>500	6, +1 space per ea. addit. 100 seats

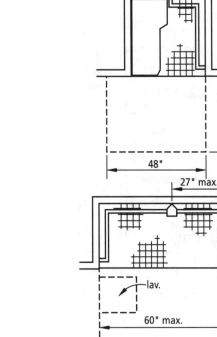

36"

36"

36"

48"

27" max.

30" min.

lav.

60" max.

36" min.

Figure 9.29
**Shower Sizes and Clearances
(36" × 36", 36" × 60").**
This material is reproduced with permission from American National Standard A117.1-1986, copyright 1986 by the American National Standards Institute. Copies of this standard may be purchased from the American National Standards Institute at 11 West 42nd Street, New York, New York 10036.

Additionally, ≥1 **percent, but** ≥1 seat(s) must be aisle seats with no armrest (or a removable armrest) on the aisle side.

(See Figure 9.39 for wheelchair space requirements.)

Medical Facilities

All new facilities and additions to and remodels of existing facilities must meet the following requirements:

Hospitals, psychiatric facilities, and detox facilities: All common/public facilities must be accessible.

≥10 **percent, but** ≥1 patient bedrooms must be wheelchair accessible **(space at doors, clear maneuvering around beds ≥36", and accessible toilet rooms and showers).**

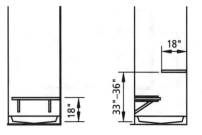

18"

18"

33"–36"

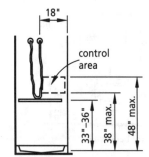

18"

control area

33"–36"

38" max.

48" max.

Figure 9.30
**Grab Bars at Shower Stalls
(36" × 36").**
This material is reproduced with permission from American National Standard A117.1-1986, copyright 1986 by the American National Standards Institute. Copies of this standard may be purchased from the American National Standards Institute at 11 West 42nd Street, New York, New York 10036.

Hospitals and rehabilitation facilities specializing in treating mobility impairments: All patient rooms and common/public areas must be accessible.

Long-term care and nursing facilities: All common/public areas must be accessible.

≥50 percent, but ≥1 patient rooms must be accessible.

Lodging Facilities

Hotels, motels, inns, and dormitories:

Exceptions: The following requirements do not apply to places accommodating ≤5 rooms for rent and the **owner resides** in the same establishment.

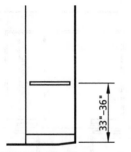
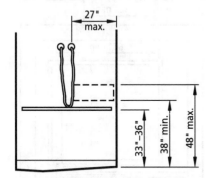

NOTE: sides similar.

Figure 9.31
Grab Bars at Shower Stalls (36" x 60").
This material is reproduced with permission from American National Standard A117.1-1986, copyright 1986 by the American National Standards Institute. Copies of this standard may be purchased from the American National Standards Institute at 11 West 42nd Street, New York, New York 10036.

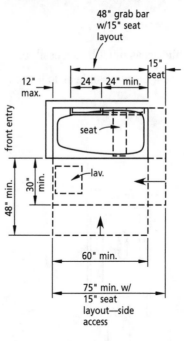

Figure 9.32
Clear Floor Space at Bathtubs.

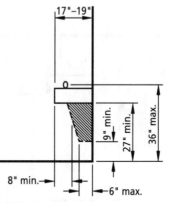

NOTE: equipment permitted in shaded area.

Figure 9.33
Spout Height and Knee Clearance at Drinking Fountain.
This material is reproduced with permission from American National Standard A117.1-1986, copyright 1986 by the American National Standards Institute. Copies of this standard may be purchased from the American National Standards Institute at 11 West 42nd Street, New York, New York 10036.

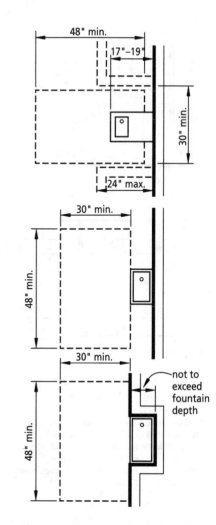

Figure 9.34
Clear Space for Drinking Fountains.
This material is reproduced with permission from American National Standard A117.1-1986, copyright 1986 by the American National Standards Institute. Copies of this standard may be purchased from the American National Standards Institute at 11 West 42nd Street, New York, New York 10036.

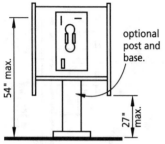

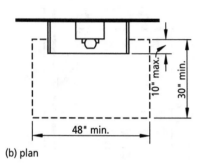

(a) elevation

(b) plan

Figure 9.35
Telephones—Side Reach Access.
This material is reproduced with permission from American National Standard A117.1-1986, copyright 1986 by the American National Standards Institute. Copies of this standard may be purchased from the American National Standards Institute at 11 West 42nd Street, New York, New York 10036.

All common/public areas must be accessible.

Sleeping rooms must be accessible as follows:

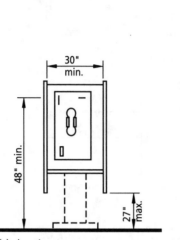

(a) elevation

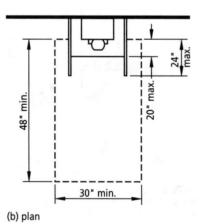

(b) plan

Figure 9.36
Telephones—Forward Reach Access.
This material is reproduced with permission from American National Standard A117.1-1986, copyright 1986 by the American National Standards Institute. Copies of this standard may be purchased from the American National Standards Institute at 11 West 42nd Street, New York, New York 10036.

# of Rooms	# of Access Rooms	Rooms w/Roll-in Showers
1–25	1	(See Figure 9.40.)
26–50	2	
51–75	3	1
76–100	4	1
101–150	5	2
151–200	6	2

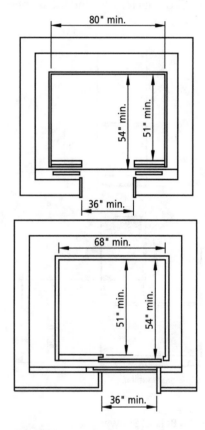

Figure 9.37
Minimum Dimensions of Elevator Cars.
This material is reproduced with permission from American National Standard A117.1-1986, copyright 1986 by the American National Standards Institute. Copies of this standard may be purchased from the American National Standards Institute at 11 West 42nd Street, New York, New York 10036.

# of Rooms	# of Access Rooms	Rooms w/Roll-in Showers
201–300	7	3
301–400	8	4
401–500	9	4 + 1 for ea. addit. 100
501–1,000	2 percent of total	
>1,001	20 + 1 for ea. addit. 100	

Accessible rooms have:

1. ≥32" clear doorways.

2. ≥36" clear accessible route to and throughout room.

3. Space at doors as required (see "Space at doors," page 105).

4. Accessible toilet rooms.

5. Accessible baths/showers.

6. Barrier-free parking as near as practical.

7. If provided, accessible kitchenettes.

Room rates: Accessible rooms must be equally available/ provided for all room classes and rates.

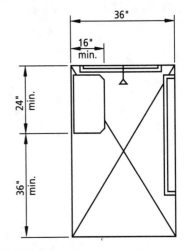

Figure 9.40
Roll-in Shower with Folding Seat.
This material is reproduced with permission from American National Standard A117.1-1986, copyright 1986 by the American National Standards Institute. Copies of this standard may be purchased from the American National Standards Institute at 11 West 42nd Street, New York, New York 10036.

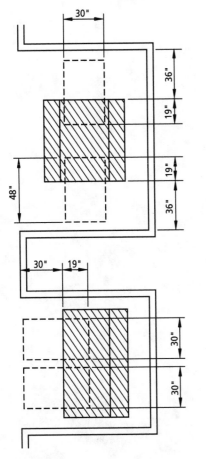

Figure 9.38
Minimum Clearance for Seating and Tables.
This material is reproduced with permission from American National Standard A117.1-1986, copyright 1986 by the American National Standards Institute. Copies of this standard may be purchased from the American National Standards Institute at 11 West 42nd Street, New York, New York 10036.

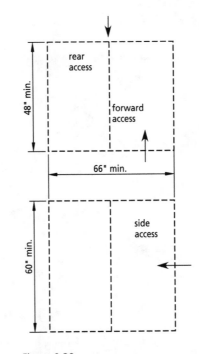

Figure 9.39
Space Requirements for Wheelchair Seating Spaces in Series.
This material is reproduced with permission from American National Standard A117.1-1986, copyright 1986 by the American National Standards Institute. Copies of this standard may be purchased from the American National Standards Institute at 11 West 42nd Street, New York, New York 10036.

113

Appendices

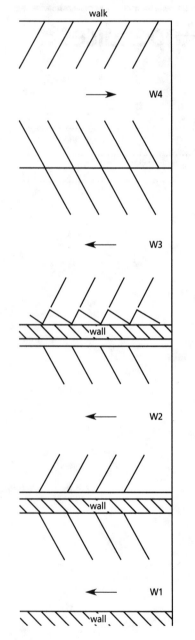

Figure A.1
Parking Stall Aisle and Width.

Table A.1   **Parking Stall and Aisle Dimensions**

Stall Width	Overall Width (W) (See Figure A.1.)	Stall Angle 45°	60°	90°
8'-0"	W1	25'-9"	29'-4"	41'-9"
	W2	40'-10"	45'-8"	57'-2"
	W3	38'-9"	44'-2"	57'-2"
	W4	36'-8"	42'-9"	57'-2"
8'-6"	W1	32'-0"	36'-2"	48'-0"
	W2	49'-10"	56'-0"	66'-0"
	W3	47'-8"	54'-0"	66'-0"
	W4	45'-2"	51'-8"	66'-0"
9'-0"	W1	32'-0"	35'-4"	48'-0"
	W2	49'-4"	55'-6"	66'-0"
	W3	46'-4"	53'-10"	66'-0"
	W4	44'-8"	51'-6"	66'-0"
9'-6"	W1	32'-0"	35'-0"	48'-0"
	W2	49'-2"	53'-6"	65'-11"
	W3	47'-0"	51'-6"	65'-11"
	W4	44'-8"	49'-10"	65'-11"

Barrier-free stalls: Minimum width: **8'-0"** + an adjacent unloading aisle ≥**5'-0"** wide.

Table B.1 **Vehicle Turning Radius and Dimensions**

Vehicle [1]	Dimensions					Turning Radius [2]
	Front Overhang	Rear Overhang	Length	Width	Height	
Passenger Car	3'-0"	3'-0"	19'-0"	7'-0"	4'-10" to 5'-4"	28'-0"
Single Unit Truck	4'-0"	6'-0"	30'-0"	8'-6"	13'-6"	45'-0"
Single Unit Bus	7'-0"	8'-0"	40'-0"	8'-6"	13'-6"	45'-0"
Articulated Bus	8'-0"	10'-0"	60'-0"	8'-6"	10'-6"	40'-0"
Semitrailer—Small	4'-0"	6'-0"	50'-0"	8'-6"	13'-6"	45'-0"
Semitrailer—Large	3'-0"	2'-0"	55'-0"	8'-6"	13'-6"	48'-0"
Semitrailer & Full Trailer Combination	2'-0"	3'-0"	65'-0"	8'-6"	13'-6"	48'-0"

1. See Figure B.1 for vehicle types.
2. See Figure B.2 for radius diagram.

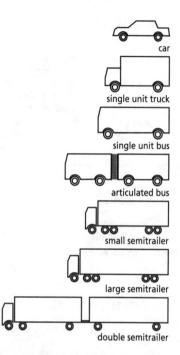

car

single unit truck

single unit bus

articulated bus

small semitrailer

large semitrailer

double semitrailer

Figure B.1
Vehicle Types.

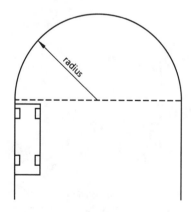

radius

Figure B.2
Turning Radius.

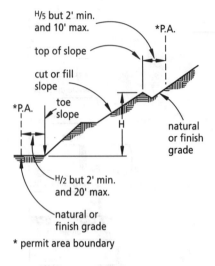

H/5 but 2' min.
and 10' max.

*P.A.

top of slope

cut or fill
slope

*P.A.

toe
slope

H

natural
or finish
grade

H/2 but 2' min.
and 20' max.

natural or
finish grade

* permit area boundary

Figure C.1
Cut and Fill Slopes [70–1].
Reproduced from the 1991 edition of the
Uniform Building Code, copyright © 1991, with
the permission of the publishers, the
International Council of Building Officials.

General Grading

Setbacks: [7011]

See Figure C.1.

Cuts: [7009]

The slope of a cut surface must be ≤**2 horizontal:1 vertical** (a steeper cut slope may be permitted by the building official if verified by a soils report).

Fills: [7010]

Fill slopes must not be constructed on natural slopes steeper than **2 horizontal:1 vertical**.

The bench under the toe of a fill on a slope steeper than **5 horizontal:1 vertical** must be ≥**10' wide**. (See Figure C.1.)

Drainage and terracing: [7012]

Terraces ≥6' wide must be established at 30' (vertical) intervals on all cut and fill slopes.

Where only one terrace is required, it must be placed at approximate mid-slope.

Where cut and fill slopes are ≥60' and ≤120' (vertical), the terrace at approximately mid-height must be ≥12' wide.

Cut and fill slopes >120' (vertical) must be designed by a civil engineer and submitted to the building official for special approval.

Swales and ditches on terraces must have a slope ≥5 percent and must be paved.